OUR GURUJI
SWAMI PURNANANDAJI MAHARAJ

AUTHOR'S NOTE

There is no published price for this book. However, if you wish to make a donation, it will be much appreciated.

Donation can be sent to:

London Sevashram Sangha
99A Devonport Road, Shepherds Bush
London W12 8PB
England.
Telephone: 020- 8743 9048
Email: sevashramvision@hotmail.com
Registered Charity Number 261363

You can use Bank transfer to:

Account Name	: **London Sevashram Sangha**
Bank	: Lloyds Bank
Account Number	: 01277340
Sort Code	: 30-94-51
BIC	: LOYDGB21318
IBAN	:GB63 LOYD 3094 5101 2773 40

Your Donation can also be given to any Bharat Sevashram Sangha Ashram of your choice. Copies of this book will be distributed to India, Guyana, Trinidad, England and North America.

A receipt and acknowledgement will be sent to you.

Kindly provide your name, address and telephone number. Copies of this book may be obtained from the London Sevashram Sangha or the Secretary, Mr. Dinesh Sukhu.

Thank you.

Girija & Dinesh

OUR GURUJI

SWAMI PURNANANDAJI MAHARAJ

Girija Gajan (previously Brahmcharie Girija)

Our Guruji Swami Purnanadaji Maharaj/ Girija Gajan

First Edition : Delhi, 2021

ISBN : 978 81 950553 1 9

Published by

MOTILAL BANARSIDASS PUBLICATIONS
93, Shyam Lal Marg, Darya Ganj, New Delhi - 110002
mlbd@mlbd.com

MLBD Cataloguing-in-Publication Data
Our Guruji Swami Purnanadaji Maharaj
by Girija Gajan
ISBN : 978 81 950553 1 9
I. Dedication II. Preface III. Acknowledgment
IV. Introducton

Printed by
Thomson Press (India) Limited (Haryana)

DEDICATION

This book is dedicated to our ever-loving grandchildren Ash and Lili Fowkes-Gajan.

CONTENTS

PREFACE

Swami Purnanandaji Maharaj was Great Master in his behavior and interactions with others. He was strong, bold, forceful and a tremendous spiritual force. He not only preached geeta attained great spiritual heights through intense sadhana. Everything I have ever achieved, and I am not far from moksha' and considred, declaired himself as Instrument of Sri Guruji Maharaj's wishes.

Swami ji was true Gyani and a monk of the highest order. He was a direct disciple of Swami Prananvanandaji Maharaj (Guru Maharajji), was the founder of Bharat Sevashram Sangha. The Sangha and future childrens of Sangha will certainly benefited from the legacy left by Guruji Swami Purnandaji Maharaj. Guruji's personality and charisma was such that all kind people were polite, respectful and hospitable. Guruji's gave us formal education, knowledge, confidence and personal beliefs, all maturing into many wonderful individual achievements. Guruji left us a legacy, tangible, spiritual and unparallel in modern times. He authored many books and articles. Bharat Sevashram Sangha Centers in Guyana, Trinidad, USA and Canada are our heritage.

He was the beginner of a momentous and historical era for the Guyanese Hindu Community. During his lecture campaign, Guruji was offered the twenty acre land by Hindu family, to establish an Ashram. In January 1956, $20.000 amount of money was offered for the construction of a large Ashram on the donated land. Hindu College was constructed on the donated land because; there were inadequate opportunities for

Hindu students, particularly from poor families, to pursue formal academic education. The introduction of the Hindu Gurukul system of education provided accommodation and a unique learning process for students all over Guyana from as far as Berbice and Essiquibo irrespective of their religious affiliation. Guruji was quick to assess the plight and needs of the Hindu community. He often remarked that formal secondary education was essential for the pride and dignity of the community to be successfully involved in the political, social economic and religious requirements of the country. There were many examples of young Hindus with adequate educational qualifications being refused a teaching job in predominantly Christian primary schools unless they converted to Christianity.

Guruji was successful in the reformation of Cremation Laws in Guyana. He had to convince the Health Minister, that it was the fundamental right of a Hindu to cremate a deceased. Moreover, cremation was cleaner and more hygienic than burial.

Constantly he worked for the welfare of hindus. Guruji was invited to Guyana by prominent Hindu leaders on a brief cultural and religious preaching mission which was expected to last for three months before he returned to Trinidad and India.

Guruji saw the needs of the Hindu community in Lonṛdon and the possibility of spreading invigorated Hinduism under the auspices of the Bharat Sevashram Sangha to the elite of London and perhaps further into Europe. Isolation from Hindu religious, cultural and social interactions also added to their dilemma to work for hindus. He spent next thirty years of his life in the services of the Hindu Communiṛty in Guyana, Trinidad, London and North America and worked tirelessly for the poor and needy. He had life changing influences on individuals and families in the Hindu and Non-Hindu communities.

On request of many dispel of Guruji, It took over ten years of research and preparation for Bhai Girija, the author of this book, who has thirteen years experience of living and working closely with Guruji in Guyana and England, has written this fascinating account of Guruji's life and work.

ACKNOWLEDGMENTS

I would like to express my thanks to many people who have contributed to the writing of this book. I am especially grateful to Dinesh and Pam Sukhu for their continual support and assistance, to Ayush and Lall Nawbatt for their encouragement and recommendations, to Mr. S.Chatterjee for information on the life of Guruji, to Mr. S.R.Sinha for securing valuable written information about Guruji°s earlier life, to Swaroop Das and Probir Sarkar for translating a document written in Bengali. I am thankful for permission to use material of tribute to Guruji from Mr. Nowrang Persaud, Dr. Lake Singh and many other prominent supporters of Guruji.

Guru Govind (previously Brahmcharie Govind) often demonstrated his brotherly love, respect and selfless support since 1955. We both owe so much to our Guruji.

We are grateful to devoted supporters of Guruji who actively offered generous and anonymous contribution.

In August 2019, I was particularly honoured by Swami Saswaknandaji Maharaj, Vice President of Bharat Sevashram Sangha, for his blessings and best wishes for the publication of this book.

My son-in-law, Dr. Robert Fowkes-Gajan who provided valuable help with formatting, editing and technical support.

I am grateful to my wife Indra for her unfailing patience and to my daughter Nadi for her support and encouragement.

INTRODUCTION

Guruji Swami Purnandaji Maharaj was a direct disciple of Bhagwan Pranavanandaji Maharaj, the founder of the Bharat Sevashram Sangha. Guruji left India and spent over thirty years of his life in continuous service for the Hindu community across the world. He established Bharat Sevashram Sangha Ashrams in Guyana, Trinidad, England and North America. He worked tirelessly for the poor and needy. He had life changing influences on individuals and families in the Hindu and non-Hindu communities.

He built the Hindu college in Cove and John, East Coast Demerara, Guyana which became the focal point of the Guyana Ashram. Later a primary school was built near the college. Under Guruji's guidance both schools proved a great success. They enabled many children from modest income families to obtain education which would have otherwise eluded them. Many of the students went on to achieve academic and professional successes in Guyana, the West Indies, England and North America.

Bhai Girja, the author of this book, has thirteen years experience of living and working closely with Guruji in Guyana and England. He has written this fascinating account of Guruji's life and work at the request of many of Guruj's disciples. It took over ten years of research and preparation.

He was the youngest of the first group of five Brahmcharies initiated by Guruji. He first met Guruji in 1955 at a Yagna in Canji, Berbice, Guyana when Guruji asked him to become his Brahmcharie.. He was immediately influenced by Guruji particularly by his endearing and fatherly manner.

Bhai Girja helped to build and establish the Ashram in Cove and John, Guyana. He later served as a teacher specializing in English and English Literature at the Hindu College and Primary school. He came to England in 1963 to assist Guruji to establish a branch of the Sangha in London. He renovated the Ashram building in Stanlake Villas, Shepherds Bush, London W12. The work involved arduous manual labour in a cold climate to which he and Guruji were unaccustomed. Bhai Girija had to attend college to learn building and technical skills up to City and Guilds standards before he could start the construction work. The renovation was completed in late 1965. The Ashram then began monthly Havan services attracting many people originally from India and the West Indies.

In 1967, Brahmcharie Girija left the monastic order. However, he maintained close links with the Sangha. He still attends services at the Ashram and gives lectures on aspects of Hinduism and Vedanta at various institutions. He has an abiding love and respect for Guruji and this book is an attempt to chart the life of our Guruji.

Dinesh Sukhu & Ayush Nawbatt

Acharya Srimat Swami Pranavanandaji Maharaj
Founder – Bharat Sevashram Sangha

Srimat Swami Purnanandaji Maharaj

Om agyaana timi raan dhasya gyann naan jana shalaa kayaa
Chak shut rumiilitam yena Tasmai Sri Gurave namah

I bow down before Gurudeva who has opened my inner vision by removing blindness of ignorance with the help of knowledge

OUR GURUJI
Sreemat Swami Purnanandaji Maharaj

THE AWRRIVAL OF GURUJI IN GUYANA

On the 28th October 1955, our Guruji, Swami Purnanandaji Maharaj stepped off the airplane at the airport in Guyana. He was greeted with the traditional Hindu devotional welcome with garlands by a large expectant group of people. Guruji approached the crowd with a beaming smile and prayer clasped hands. Thus began a momentous and historical era for the Guyanese Hindu Community.

Guruji was invited to Guyana by prominent Hindu leaders on a brief cultural and religious preaching mission which was expected to last for three months before he returned to Trinidad and India. He subsequently spent the next thirty years of his life in the services of the Hindu Community in Guyana, Trinidad, London and North America.

His mission to the West Indies started in 1950 as a deputy leader of a preaching group with Swami Advaitanandaji Maharaj as leader and two Brahmcharies, Rajkrishna and Mritunjoy. The mission was commissioned by The Bharat Sevashram Sangha and sanctioned by Pandit Nehru, Prime Minister of India, to visit Trinidad and Guyana and provide cultural and religious assistance to the Hindu community. Prior to this mission, Mr Bidesaur, a prominent Hindu leader in Trinidad went to India to solicit a professional Hindu teacher and reformer to assist the Hindu community in Trinidad. His quest eventually fell on the shoulders of the Bharat Sevashram Sangha, an organization of selfless and dedicated Sanyasis, founded by His Holiness Srimat Swami Pranavanandaji Maharaj.

Guruji arriving in Guyana for the first time

A BRIEF NOTE ON ACHARYA PRANAVANANDAJI MAHARAJ

Acharya Swami Pranavanandaji Maharaj is regarded by devotees as the incarnation of Lord Shiva. His father was a great devotee of Lord Shiva. He was faced with a series of personal danger, social and political difficulties as well as religious injustices. He undertook a year- long penance of propitiating Lord Shiva by mediation and prayers. Lord Shiva answered his devotions and promised to incarnate Himself as his son. Soon a son was born to the family of Sri Bishnu Charan Das on the auspicious day of Maghi Purnima in the year 1896.

His boyhood was spent continually in deep mediation and self contemplation, having no desire for food or play. He survived on a few handfuls of cooked rice and boiled potatoes. He avoided rich and palatable dishes. Even with this basic diet, he undertook heavy physical exercise with huge clubs and acquired uncommon and powerful strength. As he grew older, he meditated deeply and continuously. His sharp discrimination and total dispassion reminded people of two great prophets – Lord Budha and Achyara Shankara. Eventually people were convinced that he was indeed the incarnation of Lord Shiva.

In 1916, on the auspicious Maghi Purnima day, Acharya Guru Maharaj attained Divine Illumination and founded the organization – The Bharat Sevashram Sangha. Hundreds of selfless young men rallied under the banner of the Divine Acharya in connection with humanitarian, spiritual, moral, educational, religious and social activities. Guru Maharaj then began to mould the lives of some young apostles into devoted, dedicated, self-sacrificing and hard working sanyasis. Our Guruji was among the first group of twelve apostles. A comprehensive book on the life of Guruji Maharaj, Acharya Pranavanandaji was written by our Guruji, entitled 'The Prophet of the new Hindu Age'. I recommend you read this book to learn more about Guruji Maharaj and to supplement your appreciation of our Guruji.

One of the principal functions of The Bharat Sevashram Sangha was that its monks should reach out to Hindus all over India as well as other countries where a Hindu community existed. The Bharat Sevashram Sangha had been conducting preaching missions since 1929 in Burma, Malaysia, and Singapore. The outbreak of World War II in1939 halted overseas missions. In 1948, the activities resumed with ten monks under the leadership of Swami Advaitanandaji Maharaj to East African territories, Hong Kong, The Philipines and Australia.

On the 11th September 1950, Swami Advaitanandaji led the mission to the West Indies as mentioned earlier. The preaching party of four visited Mauritius, Cape Town in South Africa and Barbados and conducted lectures and meetings before arriving in Trinidad on the 28th December 1950. After eight months of missionary work in Trinidad, the group went to Guyana on the 14th September 1951 without our Guruji, who remained in Trinidad to continue with Sangha activities. The preaching group was equally successful in Guyana as it was in Trinidad with its activities well documented elsewhere.

Brahmacharie Rajkrishna, Swami Purnanandaji, Swami Advaitanandaji, Brahmacharie Mritunjoy

The purpose of undertaking this work is to illustrate the greatness of our Guruji, Swami Purnanandaji Maharaj. He was a unique sanyasi of the Bharat Sevashram Sangha.

He demonstrated immense spiritual enlightenment, unbridled enthusiasm and determination. He walked tall and briskly often with an aura of powerful and fierce energy while showing a loving and endearing personality. Above all was his enduring passion to follow the principles laid down by Sri Guru Pranavanandaji Maharaj in the service of Hinduism and the Hindu community.

Many devotees and disciples of Guruji requested me to write about Guruji and his work in Guyana and London following a few brief talks I gave on the occasion of his birth anniversary celebration in London. It was also my intention to write about my personal experiences with our Guruji particularly during the inception years of the Guyana and London Ashrams. On the 25th March 2015, I was finally persuaded to write about our Guruji following a long telephone conversation with a discipline of Guruji from Canada. She is the daughter of Mr. Ramdhani Bahadur of Canje, Berbice, Guyana, and wanted to know about her father's dedicated support to Guruji and about Guruji himself.

She was a very young girl when she was initiated by Guruji and now has very limited knowledge of Guruji and his work. I feel there are many disciples of Guruji who may have similar request.

Hopefully, I can satisfy both sentiments by relating my personal experiences of living and working with Guruji in Guyana and London and the influences he had on my life and the lives of thousands of people.

Guruji's earlier disciples will remember and share my experiences and may recollect their own relationship with our Guruji. Their children and grandchildren will proudly appreciate the valuable contribution to Guruji and the Bharat Sevashram Sangha made by their parents. The younger generation of supporters of the Bharat Sevashram Sangha particularly in London, Guyana, Trinidad and North America may learn about the pioneering and foundation work of Guruji. His saintly personality evoked devotion and dedication from many people in countries mentioned above. I have referred to some of these personalities who provided continual and obedient assistance to Guruji. The immense successes of Guruji's missionary work were largely due to the support of these people and their families. I also hope that my account of Guruji's work will help to preserve the memory of a great man and a saint.

EARLY DAYS OF GUYANA ASHRAM AND THE HINDU COLLEGE

Dr. Bahadur Singh, Pandit S. Sharma, Mr. Sugrim Singh, Mr. Budhu and Mr. Kedar, were some of the Hindu leaders who invited and welcomed Guruji to Guyana in 1955. They arranged a series of lectures and Yagna ceremonies for Guruji throughout Guyana. Originally Guruji resided at Pandit Sharma's home in Kitty, Georgetown. A memorable occasion was the Gita Yagna at the Campleville Hindu Temple attended by large crowds of people on each day of the two-week programme. The total voluntary monetary collection was offered to Guruji as was traditionally given to the presiding pandit or priest. Guruji declined the offer and gave the considerable collection of money to the management committee of the temple to use for refurbishment or upkeep of the building.

A group of the first Sangha Swamiji Maharaj. From left to right: Atmaswaruppanandaji, Purnanandaji {Guruji}, Vedanandaji, Yatishwaranandaji, Advaitanandaji, Vikashanandaji

A group of the first Sangha Swamiji Maharaj. From left to right: Omkaranandaji, Yoganandaji, Vedanandaji, Vijnanandaji, Guruji.

A group of the first Sangha Swamiji Maharaj. From left to right:
Standing back row: unknown, Br. Surah, unknown, Ramananandaji, unknown.
Standing second row: Vijoyanandaji, Jotirmayanandaji, Trilokanandaji, unknown, unknown, Radhakamatanandaji, Kanhainandaji, Ournanandaji (Guruji), Nikhilanandaji, Shiveshanandaji, Pamkojanandaji, Tyagiswaranandaji
Sitting second row: Omkaranandaji, Yoganandaji, Vedanandaji, Vijanandaji, Prajnanandaji
Sitting front row: unknown, Viswanandaji, Siddheswaranandaji, Br. Shibu, Owrupanandaji

These photographs of the early Holy Fathers show utmost simplicity , surrender, serenity, dedication and devotion to Acharya Guruji Maharaj. It is comforting to see our Guruji among them, reflecting his earlier Sangha life.

During his lecture campaign, Guruji was offered the twenty acre land in Cove & John, East Coast, Demerara by Mr. and Mrs Resaul Maharaj, a devoted and prominent

Hindu family, to establish an Ashram. In January 1956, Mr. Soogrim Persaud, a member of the Resaul family, subsequently offered a large amount of money, $20.000, for the construction of a large building on the donated land. This building was later to be popularly known as the Hindu College. Guruji was presented with a dilemma. He was expected to return to Trinidad to complete his mission there before returning to India. Guruji consulted and submitted his plans to Sangha Headquarters in Calcutta for the establishment of a Bharat Sevashram Sangha branch Ashram in Guyana. I believe this was the first Sangha branch Ashram outside of India. Permission was granted and Guruji set about raising funds and making plans for this daunting project.

The donated land was a veritable swamp island encircled by a moat like canal that received natural drainage water from the Cove & John and surrounding districts. At the narrow end of the pear shaped land, was a water pumping station used for pumping excess water from the canal through a manually operated 'koker' or barrier into the Atlantic ocean.

This koker was located on the wider end of the land. During the rainy season and at low tides, it was opened by the use of winches and pulleys and closed before the return of high tides. The Atlantic sea is on the South Eastern side of this part of the coastal area and is approximately eight feet below sea level. A high embankment of compacted earth provided some protection against flooding from the ocean. Access to the Ashram land was by a shared narrow burnt clay road from the main trunk road. The Cove & John area and neighbouring districts of Nabaclis and Enmore had a mixed race population with a majority of Hindus. During the rainy season the land became a shallow grassy and swampy lake and during the dry period it became a grazing pasture for cattle and sheep. One had to wade across the surrounding canal to reach this totally barren land.

Guruji stoically accepted the donations and the enormous challenge of starting an Ashram in Guyana. He literally embraced the land and the pioneering ordeal he was to endure as the wishes of Sri Guruji Maharaj. He moved out of the relatively agreeable accommodation of Pandit Sharma's home and lived in a nearby shed used to store coconut of a local plantation. Mr.Doodnauth, a dedicated devotee of Guruji, visited Guruji in this hovel and was shocked to learn that Guruji survived on food of raw coconut and boiled plantain leaves. Eventually, Guruji moved to the donated land and lived in a 'cow shed' type of accommodation constructed by some devotees. It was an oblong "upturned V' shaped hut made from 'wattle' tree stakes and coconut branches. He used a donated canoe type boat to cross over the canal to his sanyasi abode. Guruji went about raising money. He begged and implored people while submitting his detailed plans for his visionary and pioneering work. He held meetings and conducted several Yagnas in many districts particularly in Berbice to obtain donations and support from local as well as prominent people and institutions.

Eventually on the 26th February 1956, four months after obtaining the land, Guruji organised a ceremony for the formal laying of the cornerstone of the Dormitory and Hindu College by the Governor General, Sir Patrick Muir Renison. Local dignitaries and proud Hindus were present to witness the ceremony. Later a strong and permanent wooden bridge was constructed across the canal from the new extended road. The building materials were donated by Mr.Toolsie Persaud. Fresh water was provided to the Ashram from the public mains supply. The underground clay pipe was extended above water level across the canal near the bridge. Mrs Sahawine donated the cost of the material. Guruji often refused monetary donation, particularly for major projects. He requested the donor to pay for and supply the necessary material. In this way there was evidence that the donation was being used effectively.

Guruji with Sir Patrick Renison crossing the canal to lay cornerstone for the Hindu College in 1956.

Guruji secured the services of four professional building contractors from Trinidad to build the Dormitory and college. Mr. Kaka and Mr. Basraj headed the team. These gentlemen were devotees of Guruji and had done building work for him in Trinidad.

Construction of the building foundation began and every aspect of the work had to be done manually with basic tools. Mechanical or electrical equipment were unavailable. Various huts and sheds were built to provide basic living cooking and toilet facilities for contractors and workers. Mr. Griggs, a generous and devoted Afro-Trinidadian gentleman, donated a blue Volkswagen Beatle car to Guruji. This vehicle enabled Guruji to travel around in Guyana to conduct his Ashram work.

As the work progressed at a feverish rate, more and more people began to realize that Guruji was a special missionary sanyasi and a visionary. They rallied to offer various forms of support and more importantly was their selfless dedication and devotion. Guruji then decided to recruit young men as Brahmcharies and resident Ashram workers.

In October 1951, Swami Advaitanandaji Maharaj and Brahmcharies Rajkrishna and Mritunjoy were conducting a ceremony at the Temple in Canje, Berbice. A few friends and I were walking on the road near the temple full of worshippers and crowds of people were on the road and surrounding area. I witnessed in awe Brahmcharie Rajkrishna performing Guru Arti and sung by Mritunjoy. The sound and scene haunted me for weeks. Although I did not realize at the time, the experience had a profound and everlasting effect on my life. Prior to this incident, I knew very little about Hinduism, never visited a temple, hardly ever consciously prayed or interacted socially with any Hindus. Living conditions and circumstances did not allow for such experience.

The Canje Hindu temple became a Sangha 'Milan Mandir' as we know it today and managed by a group of local Hindu leaders with Havan and Artie services every Sunday evenings. Mr. Ramdhani Bahadur, a devoted supporter of Guruji, headed the local Milan temple administration. I gradually began to attend temple ceremonics and sat unobtrusively at the back of the temple. Mr. Bahadur and his close friend Mr. Bissundy Ragubeer approached me and encouraged me to join in more actively in temple activities. Eventually I learnt Bhajans, Havans and conducted services occasionally. I privately conducted early Sunday morning Artie in the temple and prepared the Altar for the Sunday evening public service. A building was in the process of construction near the temple for a Hindi school and to supplement other temple activities. Mr. Gaffoor, 'Skipper' a small building contractor and my 'boss' volunteered his expertise and took charge of the project. This Muslim gentleman was highly respected in the community and I personally owed him and his family a debt of gratitude for his assistance and kindness. He mustered volunteers to work at weekends to complete the construction. The influence of the Sangha Milan Mandir with the blessings of Sri Guruji Maharaj was already having an unconscious effect.

In late 1956, Guruji was conducting a Gita Yagna in the Canji temple. I was in attendance among a large crowd of people and sat at the back of the temple. At the end of the ceremony, Guruji asked Mr. Bahadur for me to go and meet him. I paid my obeisance to Guruji and he eventually asked me to go with him to the Cove and John Ashram and become a Brahmchari. I must have said 'yes'. He said he would collect me the following morning at an appointed location near the temple. There was little time to inform family and friends. I hurriedly resigned my employment with Mr. Gafoor. My younger brother and sister-in-law were shocked and upset at my sudden departure. I left with few basic clothing that could fit in a large carrier bag and no money. It was meant to be a complete surrender of worldly possessions and attachments.

At approximately 10.00am on a November day 1956, I waited alone by the side of the main road when Guruji arrived in his Volkswagen car to pick me up for the long journey to Cove and John. The car was already full with bags of donated rice and fresh vegetables along with two young Brahmchari recruits, Bhima Singh and Panday from the Albion districts. I remember clearly Guruji's beaming and welcoming smile as we were tightly bundled into the car. The journey was long and tiring from Canje across the Berbice river and along the West and East coast road to the Ashram in Cove and John. We made a few stops for Guruji to visit Sangha devotees and for us to stretch our cramped legs. Guruji would initiate casual conversations with us and we responded with 'yes or no Guruji'. I guess we were too awe struck on our journey into the unknown. Eventually we arrived at the Ashram late at night. It was too dark to fully observe our new surroundings. We received a warm welcome by a few Brahmcharies and workers who carried paraffin lanterns. We waded through ankle deep water to reach a communal shed. The shed stood on twelve inches high concrete blocks and floored with loose timber boards. The roof and walls were temporarily constructed with corrugated zinc roofing sheets and strapped together with ropes on a wooden framework. Nails were not used because all the materials were needed for the construction of the Hindu College building. At one end of this shed was Guruji's tiny partitioned sleeping space. We were offered a quick meal and advised to get some sleep.

We slept on the floor with make shift bedding materials. Brahmcharies Govind, Suryaram, Seecharan and Jaikaran shared our cramped sleeping quarters. We subsequently used this shelter for several months until the Dormitory building was completed. My first night was restless with countless thoughts and expectations. Flooded water gently lapped under the floorboards and water insects searching for dry area shared our sleeping quarters. We were awakened by the rays of the early morning sun darting through gaps in the shed. The sun rose slowly out of the Atlantic Ocean and spread its warmth and dazzling brightness over the Ashram. The soft sound of the gentle waves of the Ocean, the smell of the salty sea air and even the aroma of rotted swamp vegetation presented a calm, peaceful and sanctified atmosphere.

The immediate task was the construction of the College. The building plans showed a structure with two floors to facilitate adequate classrooms and living accommodation for Dormitory boys and Brahmcharies. It measured one hundred feet long and thirty feet wide.

All the Brahmcharies, resident paid construction workers, local volunteers and supporters worked continually and feverishly under the constant supervision of Guruji. Financial constraints necessitated manual preparation of some building materials like concrete building blocks, steel rings to secure steel rods for concrete foundations and pillars. All concrete and mortar preparation were done manually with basic tools. Tons of soil were transported, often by wheel barrow, from other parts of the land to raise the floor level of the ground floor for eventual concreting and screed. The major outer shell construction work took several months before the start of other work of wall rendering, roof construction, several windows and doors installation and one external stairway and one internal stairway to the upper floor. Late night work was occasional and was done by the use of several paraffin lanterns or pumped pressurized gas lamps. There was no electricity supply.

Constant hard manual work was physically very exhausting. Guruji insisted we ate regular meals and rested as necessary. Occasionally, he worked with us at mixing concrete, pushing loaded wheel borrows and making concrete building blocks. He joked that he had done this kind of work in the Ashrams in India and that he was fully experienced in construction requirements. During the early days of the London Ashram, Guruji manually worked much harder and more frequently often suffering bruised and blistering hands. He would often share a joke and a laugh with people around him. This did help to relieve tiring and tense situations. Once while we were compacting or ramming down earth around the base foundation of the college building, Brahmchari Bheema shouted out 'Ram Ram bhaijee, Guruji is coming'. Later Guruji smilingly said, 'I heard that'. Guruji's love and concern for the people around him would often be repeated in this way.

Guruji eventually moved out of the communal hut. Brahmcharies and devotees built a 'cow shed' type construction on a higher piece of ground near the bridge across the canal. It was an oblong hut made from sturdy tree branches as posts on two sides to support the inverted 'V' shaped roof sloping on both sides to within eighteen inches of the ground. The long side walls and roof were covered and thatched with branches of coconut trees. The front and rear ends were left partially open for ventilation. It measured approximately ten feet long and five feet wide. Guruji requested this type of accommodation for his house and office. He resided in this hut for a considerable period and well after the College and Dormitory building was completed. Here at least he had some measure of privacy but was uncomfortably exposed to the elements. He also had to tolerate nightly visits from mosquitoes, swamp flies and other insects.

Cooking and sleeping facilities for workers and some Ashram residents were built with similar material. The cooking stove was a large 'chulha' made from concrete blocks and firewood was used for fuel. Once the cooking enclosure went up in flames as the open fire was blown onto the coconut branches. Lavatory facility was a tall wooden squared box with a zinc sheet roof cover measuring approximately four feet by four feet. It rested on a wooden shuttle box holed in the ground and raised to suitable height to prevent flooded water entering the toilet pit. It had a wooden seat with a convenient hole in the centre. A few external steps and a wooden or zinc door provided access and privacy. This outhouse construction was common in the district. Later, more were built to provide facilities for College and Primary School students.

FIRST GROUP OF BRAHMCHARIES IN GUYANA

There were six initiated Brahmcharies around this early period. Jaikaran and Suryaram were initiated in August 1956 at the Ashram in Cove and John. Govind and Seecharan were initiated in November 1956 on the beaches in Portmaurant, Berbice. Bheema and Girija were initiated in December 1956 at the Ashram in Cove and John. Novice Brahmcharies were Panday, Paul and Raja. Although the major work was the construction of the Hindu College and Dormitory for boys, there were other associated tasks and duties to be undertaken by the Brahmcharies and resident workers.

An effective drainage system was necessary to deal with the barren swampy land. A series of herringbone trenches were dug out to drain the frequently flooded water into the surrounding canal. Brahmcharies and Ashram workers completed the work manually with the use of basic tools like shovels and spades. The Brahmcharies took turns in cooking, washing cooking utensils, cleaning toilets and tidying surrounding areas. Periodically, they foraged for firewood for cooking from the land of local supporters of Guruji.

Financial anxiety weighed heavily on Guruji. Although monetary donations for building materials were promised, they were slow to mature. Guruji then decided to fast for however long it took until the promised donation was given. Eventually the donor respectfully apologized to Guruji and the donation was offered to facilitate continued building progress.

Guruji conducted long Yagna services particularly at the Nigg, Portmaurant and Canji districts in Berbice to raise money for the project in Cove and John. He traveled to other parts of Guyana along the East and West coasts of Demerara as well as in Georgetown and suburban districts conducting smaller meetings and discussions to raise awareness and funds for his pioneering work in Cove and John.

Brahmcharies: Govind, Girija and Seecharan

Brahmcharies: Seecharan and Girija

Guruji identified and used the skills his Brahmcharies brought with them. Brahmcharie Govind and Brahmcharie Suryaram were proficient tailors. Guruji invested in a few pedal sewing machines and associated tailoring requirements.

These Brahmcharies set about making suits, shirts and trousers for local clothing shops. This small industry helped to provide some income for the Ashram. Brahmcharies Seecharan and Girija learnt a bit about sewing and soon became good at sewing buttons on garments. Kurtas and dhotis for Guruji and Brahmcharies were made by this industry. Many people know the story of Guruji's request for his clothing and more noticeable his kurta, should be made from used flour sacks. It was made as requested by this tailoring group. There will be many more examples of Guruji's carefulness with Ashram finance and more particularly his reluctance to spend money on his personal needs.

Brahmcharie Girija had some basic carpentry and building experience. Brahmcharies Suryaram and Seecharan were strong body builders. These three Brahmcharies were an asset to the professional builders particularly for heavy building work. Brahmcharie Jaikaran was smaller in stature, fair skin and handsome. He was full of joviality and pranks but he got stuck in and provided support with all tasks. One of Guruji's devotees loaned us a tractor with a trailer to help with transportation of building materials. Brahmcharie Jaikaran boasted that he could drive the vehicle. We protested against his intention, but he quickly jumped onto the tractor, started the engine and drove the tractor into the nearby canal much to our horror and anxiety. Luckily he came out unharmed and no damage was done to the tractor.

There was no temple for worship and services. There was no facility for Artie or prayer. Brahmcharies individually practiced disciplines of jap, mediation and yoga between the hours of 4.00 am and 6.00 am daily for their spiritual development. Academic studies were done in the evening whenever possible. Brahmcharies and resident workers needed to be ready soon after 6.00 o'clock in the morning for a full days building work and other Ashram duties every day. Whenever convenient, we demonstrated our respect and obeisance to Guruji particularly when meeting him for the first time in the morning. Spiritual lessons of patience, obedience, dedication, and steadfastness were practiced and obtained through sheer dedicated work and service. This was one of the lessons given by Sri Guruji Maharaj. A similar work ethic was necessary and experienced during the first three years of establishing the London Sevashram Sangha. This will later be described in detail.

As the college building work was near completion, Guruji began preparation for the formal opening of the Hindu College. He traveled frequently to meet with heads of Secondary Schools and other academic professionals for advice and recommendations. Major and detailed consideration had to be given to the following:

1. Classroom design and facilities. Benches and writing desks for students, tables and chairs for teachers, chalkboards and classroom partitions were made locally by Mr. Doodnauth, Girija and other Ashram helpers.
2. Recruitment of teachers.
3. Teaching curriculum.
4. Liaison with relevant Government Departments.

5. Plans for the opening ceremony.
6. Advertising the occasion in the National newspapers and printing effective fliers.
7. Preparation for Secondary School application, Entry test examination and offer of Scholarships.
8. Advertising the 'Gurukul' system of education and preparation for boy's Dormitory facilities.
9. Identification of districts to be targeted for house to house visits and distribution of leaflets and fliers by Brahmcharies and Ashram workers.

Guruji planned, supervised and managed the above and many more associated projects by himself. It must be remember that Guruji was a Bharat Sevashram Sangha Sanyasi in the truest and strictest sense. Yet, he demonstrated effective secular skills in project and people management.

In March 1957, Guruji publicly announced a projected date of 8th April 1957 for the formal opening of the College and Dormitory. Guruji also advertised that a Temple at the Ashram would be opened at the same time although there was no evidence of a Temple being constructed. Many people felt that it was impossible to achieve both predictions. However, devotees from Nigg, Albion and Portmaurant districts of Berbice promised Guruji to build the Temple at the Ashram. Guruji's faith in his devotees was justified. These supporters could not afford the time for several days work at the Ashram. They prepared a prefabricated structure in Berbice during their spare time, transported it and eventually erected the Temple at the Cove and Ashram well ahead of the opening ceremony. This spirited dedicated work for Guruji was frequently repeated by his disciples and supporters.

The College building structure was at this time a construction outer shell with a roof. Everyone had to work harder and faster to achieve the deadline. Working during the night became necessary. I remember nailing down green-heart tongue and grove timber flooring of the first Dormitory floor up to 3.00 A.M. We all worked frantically to complete the task with Guruji supervising and manually supplying flooring timber and nails. I did not think anyone felt tired. We were encouraged by Guruji's presence and occasional jokes and smiling face. These dedicated and enthusiastic work ethics were prevailing aspects of Ashram life. Few hours of sleep and rest were only a physical necessity.

Guruji organized and conducted a 'Gita Yagna' for six days at the Ashram. A temporary canopied tent was erected for the ceremony. There were three important reasons for this large public occasion:

Raising funds and public awareness of construction progress.

Announcing the date for the opening ceremony of the College.

Initiating two novice Brahmcharies formally.

Standing: Builders from Trinidad Sitting: Bheema and Girija

Brahmcharies Girija and Bheema were initiated according to Vedic rites and put on saffron robes the first time. Prior to this ceremony, they wore white Kurta and Dhotie as novitiate after Guruji had given them a mala and a Jap mantra respectively soon after they joined the Ashram. The Brahmcharya initiation ceremony was elaborate with hundreds of people observing it possibly for the first time. We fasted for the day. Our heads were shaven. We took bath and were wrapped loosely in a simple white cloth. Later we were presented to Guruji who waited patiently to perform the ceremony during an arranged interval of the Yagna. He had previously announced the ceremony to a large gathering of people in attendance for the GitaYagna. They watched silently and in rapt attention. Guruji and his two disciples were in full view of everyone but out of hearing distance of the communication between Guruji and his disciples. Guruji then gave each of us a saffron robe and a beggar's walking staff. He instructed a male attendant to dress us accordingly. We returned to Guruji individually when he placed the sacred cord around our shoulder and whispered the sacred mantra in our ear. We had to repeat the mantra several times to assure Guruji that we recited it correctly. Guruji then gave us the Rudraksha mala and instructed us how to use it. He explained the importance of the initiation and the significance of the saffron robe, the sacred cord, the beggar's staff, the mala and the sacred mantra. Guruji then provided the audience with a brief explanation of this ancient Vedic initiation ceremony. Few women devotees were in tears and at the time we could not understand the reason for such reaction.

Girija and Bheema

We were expected to walk around in this outfit for sometime. There was no public celebration but you could feel the warm welcome and congratulation from the other Brahmcharies and Ashram workers. This day was to become a singularly memorable occasion for us and perhaps for other Brahmcharies as well. Guruji's fatherly assurance and pride was evident through a smiling countenance. He had taken on an eternal and enormous responsibility for his Brahmcharies.

The saffron kurta and dhoti worn by Brahmcharies and Swamijis is the dress code for The Bharat Sevashram Sangha. The kurta is full sleeved, long tailed, collar less shirt with few buttons below the neckline. The dhoti is a long, ankle length, barrel skirt type robe and wide enough for walking strides and sitting on the floor. It is often folded in front and tied around the waist with a cloth string. Perhaps I should explain the need to wear this saffron robe.

The reason for wearing the robe was best described by Guruji when an English gentleman in London asked him why he was dressed in the saffron robe. Guruji replied that his dress indicated that he was a 'dead man'. Hence the article in the Guyana Chronicle about Guruji's work in London headlined " Dead man Walking". Guruji further explained that the robe indicated that he had renounced any personal need for physical or material comforts. These sentiments had been 'cremated'. The saffron or ochre colour represented the sacred flame of the cremation fire.

THE GURUKUL SYSTEM OF EDUCATION

The Brahmchari initiation ceremony was an aspect of the Vedic Gurukul system of education. It is as old and eternal as Hinduism itself. Our Vedas, the Mahabarat, the Upanishads and the Puranas are full with examples of Gurukul education. Guruji's Hindu College and Dormitory were expected to incorporate aspects of the Gurukul system of education. It basically means that the teacher (the Guru} and the student live together and the student learns by serving and observing. Knowledge is transmitted through hard work, dedication, respect and obedience. The constant fatherly presence of the Guru evokes assurance and confidence. The Guru facilitates academic as well as spiritual education. He provides opportunities to develop skills for effective management of family, social and religious affairs. The student will then be equipped with the required knowledge to carry out his expected duties respectfully and successfully.

Guruji attracted a large number of Sangha supporters and helpers of different categories and attributes. They offered land and monetary donations, clothes and food. They provided manual assistance, construction advice and special skills. Their selfless dedication, love and respect for Guruji was constant without question. Among some families, discussion or a thought about Guruji and the Ashram was a regular feature in their daily life. The Sangha became an important influence and part of their family. This bonding initiated since the early nineteenth fifties, continues today with succeeding generations.

Mr. Doodnauth was such a devoted worker for Guruji especially during this frantically demanding period. His love for Guruji was constant and unfaltering. Every request by Guruji for his service was immediately obeyed. Mr. Doodnauth and his equally devoted wife, Mrs Rukmin Doodnauth, with a family of four young children lived in Cambelville near Georgetown about sixteen miles from the Cove and John Ashram. His frequent journey to the Ashram and endless time spent on manual, carpentry and other building work demonstrated his love and respect for Guruji. His selfless dedication must have had some strain on his family. This tall, slim, quiet and unobtrusive gentleman was much respected and appreciated by all who had some association with the Ashram. In 1980, Guruji referred to Mr. Doodnath as 'a great soul'. I mention Mr. Doodnauth now because I will on many more instances refer to his contribution to Guruji and the Cove and John Ashram. I personally worked with him on many occasions and learnt a lot from his carpentry, plumbing and other building skills. He showed genuine and sincere respect for all the Brahmcharies and workers in the Ashram.

Gradually the construction progressed on schedule. By the blessings of Sri Guruji Maharaj there was no accident and no one was seriously ill or injured despite the precarious and sometimes dangerous working conditions. Timber scaffolding up to the roof of the building was basic and often so unstable that one expected it to collapse at any time. Nailing down corrugated zinc roofing sheets and panels was dangerous without any safety measures. This type of risks that Guruji had undertaken was repeated on many occasions particularly during the early stages of building the London Sevashram Sangha.

Eventually the Hindu College building work was completed and the Trinidadian contractors returned home. Guruji then advertised in the national newspapers the formal opening of the Hindu College and the new Hindu temple to take place on the 8th April 1957. Fliers and leaflets were printed and distributed to local and neighbouring districts by Brahmcharies and Ashram workers. Formal invitations were sent to dignitaries and prominent people. Guruji took Mr. Doodnauth and myself to visit secondary schools in Georgetown, particularly Guyana Oriental College and Queen's College, to observe classroom layouts. We took measurements of desks, benches, tables, blackboards and partitions with the hope of copying the designs and making the classroom facilities ourselves. Guruji bought the required materials and tools. We set about making the furniture immediately. Again we had set targets and had to work frantically hard and long hours to complete all requirements before the proposed date for the opening of the Hindu College.

The Brahmcharies moved their living accommodation to the sectioned off part of the upper floor of the building. They used the external stairway as entrance from the northern side. Guruji continued to reside in the 'cow shed' hut near the bridge, unhealthily exposed to the elements, mosquitoes and swamp insects. On rainy days, it was difficult to stay dry and protect his books and office materials.

The first teacher employed by Guruji was Mr. Nowrang Persaud. Shortly afterwards Mr. Shastri Tiwari was employed. Both these young gentlemen were devoted supporters of Guruji's pioneering work. Guruji's endearing personality persuaded these teachers to take on a challenging task with no prospects of job or financial security. However, they did not have to convert to Christianity to obtain a teaching job and they were helping Guruji on a unique venture. They helped to plan the school programme and curriculum. They prepared entry tests and criteria for scholarship selection for prospective students. Later, two other teachers, Mr. Hoyte and Mr. Sancho, were added to the teaching staff.

FORMAL OPENING OF THE HINDU COLLEGE IN 1957

On the 8th April 1957, a public ceremony was held to celebrate the formal opening of the Hindu College, the Dormitory and the Temple. Mr. F D Jakeway CMG, OBE, Chief Secretary and Mr. Frank Mc David CMG, OBE, Minister of Agriculture were guest speakers. The anticipated Temple donated and completed by the devotees from Berbice, was declared opened by Mrs. Megharan Maharaj on the same day. In the evening after the formal opening ceremony, Ashram workers and devotees staged a play on aspects of the Ramayan. Reading from the Ramayan and bhajan singing were conducted by Guruji's popular musician, Mr. Manick. Brahmcharie Jaikaran was a lively contributor and Brahmcharie Suryaram demonstrated Yoga Assanas.

There were several factors that prompted Guruji to build the Hindu College. There were inadequate opportunities for Hindu students, particularly from poor families, to pursue formal academic education. Qualified teachers who declared that they were Hindus found it difficult to secure a job in some schools unless they converted to Christianity. The introduction of the Hindu Gururukul system of education provided accommodation and a unique learning process for students all over Guyana from as far as Berbice and Essiquibo irrespective of their religious affiliation. Guruji was quick to assess the plight and needs of the Hindu community. He often remarked that formal secondary education was essential for the pride and dignity of the community to be successfully involved in the political, social economic and religious requirements of the country. There were many examples of young Hindus with adequate educational qualifications being refused a teaching job in predominantly Christian primary schools unless they converted to Christianity. I personally witnessed a public protest in Canje, Berbice, when a staunch Hindu gentleman was refused a teaching post at St, Patrick's primary school unless he converted to Christianity.

There were no secondary schools between Georgetown and Rosignal, a distance of approximately seventy miles. Wealthy families could afford to send their children to secondary schools in Georgetown or New Amsterdam and often paid for their boarding facilities and accommodations. The poorer and not so well off families could not contemplate providing secondary education for their children. In some cases, even if families could afford the necessary expenses, they had reservations about the safety of their children, particularly young girls, if they had to travel long journeys or reside at accommodations away from their homes. Some families found it necessary to use the assistance of their children in farming, agriculture and domestic duties and sometimes, their help took priority over secondary education.

Guruji's Hindu College Dormitory would go a long way to remedy the situation by providing affordable and secure accommodation for students from all over Guyana. The opportunity was open to all students irrespective of their religious affiliations and was taken up by some students and a few teachers.

Guruji employed teachers of different faiths and instructed that morning school assembly and prayers should be available for Hindus, Christians and Muslims students respectively. During the early days of the College there was no Muslim teacher or available Imam to conduct prayers for Muslim students. Guruji asked Mr. Nowrang Persaud to learn some Muslim prayers from his Muslim friend. He then started to conduct the morning prayers for the Muslim students. Eventually senior and capable Muslim students took over the responsibility to conduct the morning prayers. Christian teachers, Mr. Hoyte and Mr. Sancho conducted Christian prayers for the Christian students. A Brahmcharie or senior student led the Hindu prayers for the Hindu students.

At the beginning, Guruji felt that it was expedient to name the College, Cove and John High School. Later Guruji renamed it the Hindu College and to this day that is how it is fondly and nostalgically remembered.

Although it was named Hindu College, it was a non-sectarian school providing equal opportunities for all students. However, it was a college that brought about a sense of pride for all Hindus in Guyana and its values were respected and appreciated by other religious denominations. This initiative of Guruji was perhaps the beginning of what is now popularly termed 'community cohesion'.

BRAHMCHARIES AS COLLEGE TEACHERS

Guruji wanted his Brahmcharies to be effective teachers and eventually take over the management of the Hindu College. He employed professional teachers from various colleges and institutions, including Queen's College in Georgetown, to assist with their preparation for the necessary academic and teaching qualifications. He charted out what subjects each Brahmcharie should specialize in to cover as far as possible a broad spectrum of courses the Hindu College would provide.

If it was a miracle that Guruji built and established the Hindu College in just over one year, since the corner stone was laid in February 1956 to the opening in April 1957, then the next venture was another miracle. His five initiated Brahmcharies had little or no opportunity for any formal academic education. Guruji still expected them to be qualified secondary school teachers as quickly as possible. With the blessings of Sri Guruji Maharaj and Guruji's loving encouragement and support, his Brahmcharies took the required G.C.E O' Level examinations with varying degrees of successes. The following year brought in more success for a few Brahmcharies at the G.C.E A-Level on selective subjects. After a full day of Ashram manual and other duties, the Brahmcharies study time began at 6.30 PM and can go until early next morning. As examination time drew nearer, it was not unusual for a Brahmcharie to have less than four hours sleep daily.

After the first College year, The Brahmcharies were teachers in different subjects.

Brahmcharie Govind - Mathematics and Chemistry.
Brahmcharie Seecharan - Biology.
Brahmcharie Suryaram - Mathematics and Geography.
Brahmcharie Jaikaran - Hindi and other subjects in the lower forms.
Brahmcharie Girija - English Language, English Literature, History, Religious Knowledge and Latin.

As usual with so many of his initiatives, Guruji was aware of the extraordinary risks and challenges. He knew he had to convince the other teachers, parents and students that his Brahmcharies would be competent and effective teachers. Occasionally he would stand at the back of the classroom and observe the teaching and teaching methods of his Brahmcharies. One was never sure of his motives. Was it because he wanted to ensure the class behaved properly, instill confidence in the Brahmcharie or make him nervous? He never openly complimented anyone, but you could sense his pride and satisfaction as he smiling left the classroom. My first English Literature class of senior students who were about the take their first public examination was one such incident. We were discussing a subject essay. I had prepared extensively and even thrown in a 'red herring' as I was expecting a challenging debate. A group of bright students proudly and confidently declared that my statement was incorrect.

It seemed the other students were in agreement with the lead students. Guruji stood at the back of the classroom, arms folded across his chest with an expressionless countenance. I was unsure of what he was thinking. Would he be angry if I was wrong? I asked the class to refer to a numbered page and paragraph in their text. The students eventually agreed with my conclusions particularly when I asked them to refer to previous chapter on the subject and explained why I thought they had some justification for the misunderstanding. I looked at Guruji and he looked at me and walked away smiling. It was a kind of smile one never forgets. Many of his disciples would remember him by this holy and reassuring smile.

THE DORMITORY FOR BOYS

The upper floor of the Hindu College building was partitioned into three sections: one for the Brahmcharies, the middle section for the Dormitory boys and the third for a teaching classroom with internal staircase from the ground floor. The dormitory was an open plan lodging for the boys each with his own bed, writing desk, chair and facilities for his personal belongings. Living with Guruji and the Brahmcharies, the boys were provided with the character building opportunity and experience of the Hindu way of life and spiritual values as previously described by the Gurukul system of education.

They performed communal morning and evening prayers and 'Artie', ate the same food prepared for Guruji and the Brahmcharies and attended a full day's college teaching. There were limited recreational and sports activity during the day and after school periods. Brahmcharies and teachers were often available to assist with the boys' homework. Guruji would often appear in the Dormitory to observe and support. His midnight visits ensured that the boys were safe and comfortable. Sometimes a student was fast asleep with a book on his chest. Guruji would put away the book, turn off the lamp and spread a blanket over the student.

Occasionally they helped with Ashram duties and activities. They learned and conduct Temple Services (Sandhya and Havan). They cleaned and prepare the temple for various Temple activities and occasionally accompanied Guruji and the Brahmcharies to private and public religious ceremonies. With limitations, they helped out with menial and manual work in the Ashram. Some students originated from as far as Port Maurant in Berbice and Leguan in Essiquibo. The Dormitory boys lived in the Ashram during term periods and went home during the break between school terms. Parents were allowed to visit often to provide washed garments, personal needs and their mother's home cooked food and delicacies. Discipline was strict but routine and flexible. On rare occasion when they misbehave, parents were advised. They generally supported Guruji and the Brahmcharies on any corrective actions. Many boys were initiated by Guruji as his disciples and were sons of devoted supporters of Guruji. Several young Ashram Dormitory boys progressed to be prominent and famous people in Guyana and in other countries. They continue to provide commendable contribution to society in general and have often recounted their wonderful experiences during their formative years in the Dormitory. Guruji's Gurukul system of education greatly influenced the lives of these men. It was a unique form of education and perhaps the first of its kind in the Western World.

Although there was no Dormitory for girls, they shared equal opportunities in other aspects of the Hindu way of life in education, culture and religious practices as well as in the pursuit of formal academic education. A few years later, when the Hindu temple and other facilities were available, Guruji encouraged a group of the College girls to organize and conduct Havan services for the College students on Friday afternoons. They sang Bhajans and performed Artie collectively. Occasionally Guruji would visit to give support and encouragement. Many of these young women were equally successful as the men and continued to support the Sangha activities in Guyana and other countries.

The Hindu College progresses steadily and began to receive prominent recognition, particularly as students were successful in the College of Preceptors (CP) and GCE O' level examinations. The percentage of passes was favourably comparable with that of more established secondary schools in Guyana. The overwhelming success of Guruji's pioneering work of establishing the Guyana Sevashram Sangha, of which the Hindu College was a focal achievement, was only possible because of the support and dedication of the Guyana Hindu community. Eminent personalities, the wealthy, the humble and the poor have all contributed to Guruji's achievement. Later, I feel it necessary to mention some of the remarkable, selfless and devoted assistance given to Guruji.

Guruji's attention then turned to other aspects of Ashram activities. The management of a growing number of Ashram residents required a regular cook. Guruji employed Mr. Lakshman, a local gentleman affectionately named 'Foreman'. He provided breakfast, lunch and supper for all Ashram residents. He also took on the work of cleaning classrooms, toilet facilities and the surrounding areas of the school. Brahmcharies and dormitory boys often assisted in cleaning work. It was not unusual for students who arrived early in the morning for school, to see a Brahmcharie teacher sweeping and dusting classrooms. Guruji also would occasionally be seen picking up debris and litter. This was an aspect of the Gurukul system of education.

The Temple was donated, constructed and erected by devotees of Guruji from the Nigg and Portmaurant districts in Berbice. Mr. Doodnauth, Brahmcharies and local support workers provided assistance with the construction. Later Mr. Doodnauth framed a large photograph of Sri Guruji Maharaj and built the Altar. The temple provided facility for daily worship (morning and evening Artie for Ashram residents) and Havan services for the public on Sunday mornings.

A temporary shed of corrugated zinc sheets enclosure was erected to provide cooking and dining facilities for residents and visitors. The cooking stove was large concrete ‘choola’ on compacted earth at ground level with facility for three cooking utensils and firewood was used for fuel. Foreman spent most of his cooking time squatting or sitting on the floor. Dining table and benches were roughly made from two inches by four inches ‘green heart’ wood materials left over from the Hindu College construction. To provide water supply to this building and nearby shower facilities, iron metal pipe plumbing had to be extended from the standpipe near the bridge to distance of approximately of forty feet. Guruji bought the necessary materials and tools.

Mr. Doodnauth was again the man to turn to for help. I had to learn quickly to use the plumbing tools particularly the threading auger and discs. It was a master class in plumbing provided by the indomitable Mr. Doodnauth with whom I worked at a furious pace to complete the task. A standpipe was placed near the kitchen and shower facilities were erected nearby. The shower enclosure of a few cubicles was made from corrugated zinc sheets with spaced wooden flooring for drainage. There was no roof.

As the number of students increased, another temporary building was erected near the College building to facilitate three further classrooms. Deadline was tight as usual. The weekend before the Monday start of a new school year was frantic with building of new writing desks, benches and other classroom requirements. Sunday evening saw the need for six more desks and benches. Guruji instructed that they needed to be ready by Monday morning for the arrival of new students. We need to work throughout the night for the task to be completed. Using basic carpentry tools and help from a few Brahmcharies and Dormitory students, I was expected to accomplish the work directed by Guruji. Brahmcharie Seecharan and I worked tirelessly throughout the night. Guruji helped as well. His presence gave us encouragement and added energy. At 0830, the students were arriving, just when we finished sanding the last set of furniture and placed them in classrooms. After a quick shower and breakfast, we were ready to welcome the new students and start the days teaching.

As mentioned before, the land became a flooded plain during rainy days. Guruji was advised that an effective drainage system was necessary. A herringbone pattern of trenches where smaller drains would lead into a larger one was dug out. Initially, a borrowed tractor was used for digging larger trenches and marked out the area for smaller drains. Initially, professionals were used. Later, additional irrigation work was done manually by Brahmcharies and voluntary helpers.

Guruji employed a professional carpenter team to construct a timber 'Koker' system to be operated manually for flooded water to be emptied into the canal via the embankment in front the College building. At least two kokers were necessary to irrigate the large twenty-acre land. Guruji instructed me to work with the builders and learn how to build the next and subsequent kokers. Fortunately, I had previous experience of building this type of drainage system, but on a larger scale. The contractors were annoyed when Guruji told them that they would no longer be needed to build the other kokers. A bitter and loud argument ensued with threatening gestures from one of the contractors. Brahmcharie Seecharan and myself heard the threats from a distance and were unsure how to respond. Later we regretted our naivety and inability to intervene and support Guruji.

Guruji took me along to Georgetown to purchase the required greenheart planks, timbers, bolts and tools. I started building the koker on the left side embankment near the bridge. The work could only be done at weekends and after school teaching periods.

The construction involved a large box with inner dove tailed squared timber supports to prevent cave in from earth and water pressure. It was two feet by two feet width and dept and approximately fifteen feet long. It had a slotted opening on one end for a door with a tall handle to be operated manually to allow water to drain into the canal at low tide. The door was closed at other times to prevent water from the canal entering into the trenches. This was a simple but effective irrigation system. Yet again, Mr. Doodnauth assisted whenever he could. Brahmcharie Seecharan and Dormitory boys helped with the movement of heavy material. When the construction of the box was completed, it was lowered into a channel dug out to an appropriate level for adequate drainage. This coffin like koker was then covered up with earth. All that could be seen was the mechanism to open and close the koker as necessary.

With the popular generous donation by Mrs. Mangri Sahawine, Guruji embarked on the building of a Science Laboratory for the Hindu College. Very few secondary schools in Guyana had fully equipped Science laboratories at the time. The Hindu College science laboratory would enhance the profile of the College. As usual Guruji embarked on another pioneering and risky venture. He researched the viability of a science laboratory by visiting schools and institutions and seeking professional advice and recommendations. The Principal of Queen's College in Georgetown, Mr. Sanger Davis, was particularly helpful to Guruji. I recall at least two visits by Mr. S. Davis to the Hindu College to advise on laboratory structural layout, experimental equipment and facilities. Later, this generous gentleman recommended his graduate teachers to give private tuitions to

Guruji's Brahmcharies. I personally was lucky to have tuition in English Language and English Literature at GCE A-Level from Mr. Cameron, an Oxford graduate and Head of English at Queen's College. Mrs. Cameron, a Cambridge graduate, also assisted with tuition on a Saturday mornings. These kind people were polite, respectful and hospitable. They provided their services free of charge. Such was the effect of Guruji's personality and charisma.

However, Guruji, Mr. Doodnauth and myself visited Queen's College and other schools with Science laboratories to observe and make notes on physical requirements. The laboratory was designed to be located on the ground floor of the College and occupying approximately two thirds of the ground floor area. Three large heavy tables had to be built with facilities for laboratory experiments by students. Gas Bunsen burners and water supply with all plumbing requirements of taps, sinks and drainage were necessary. Additional workstations against two walls were required for a full science classroom. The cost of building these facilities by contractors was astronomical. Guruji again asked Mr. Doodnauth to help out. He worked every hour he could spare at weekends and during school holidays. At that time, prepared wood or electrical tools were unavailable. Greenheart timber and planks were cut to size and planed manually to arrive at required surfaces. A partitioned wall was built to separate the main laboratory from the chemical storage and preparation room with safety equipment and security precautions.

Mr. Doodnauth completed the task almost by himself. Whenever time permitted after teaching periods and at weekends, I helped him with the heavy carpentry work. It was often a privilege to work with him. He was always polite and respectful to all the Brahmcharies and I believe he was also proud of us. Guruji asked Mr. Doodnauth to teach me plumbing skills in using dice to cut threads on steel pipes and joining them to elbows and connectors as well to sinks and taps in the science laboratory. The use of 'red led' as a connection sealant was a revelation. This plumbing experience was useful for other plumbing work in the Ashram. Eventually, Guruji directed that I should undertake and complete the plumbing work for the laboratory by myself with occasional assistance from Brahmcharie Seecharan and Mr. Doodnauth. A channel on the concrete floor under each laboratory table was cut to conceal pipe work for water supply and drainage by using basic hammer and chisel and other manual implements.

There was a memorable incident while I was working in the Laboratory. I was lying on my back on the concrete floor covered in grease and dirt and trying to connect a sink trap under a table. A gentleman standing over me remarked that I was dirty and I should go and get cleaned up. He was a familiar but pompous supporter of Guruji among a group of distinguished visitors escorted by Guruji. I was livid. I crawled out of my cramped position and failing to attack him verbally and perhaps physically, I offered him the heavy wrench and asked him to do the plumbing work and stay clean. I then threw the wrench against a wooded partition and stormed away very angry. Everybody expected Guruji, at best, to give me a serious telling off. He never did. Later, he consoled me by saying that I was tired and that the gentleman should not have made such a remark. He then smiling told me to go and repair the damaged partition. Guruji must have apologized to this distinguished gentleman on my behalf. This was our Guruji showing understanding, empathy and support.

The Science Laboratory was completed and formally opened on the 2nd February 1959 by Governor Sir Patrick Renison at a public ceremony. Three years earlier, Sir Patrick Renison had laid the corner stone of the Hindu College Building. Among other dignitaries was Guruji's friendly supporter and advisor, Mr. Sanger Davis.

MR. GRIGGS, PROMINENT SUPPORTER FROM TRINIDAD

Mr. Griggs, a prominent Trinidadian of African origin, was a staunch supporter of Guruji and his work in Trinidad. He sponsored and published two books written by Guruji when he was in Trinidad. The first was a book on Yoga courses and the second was the Bhagwat Gita, which was published in September 1955. Both books were written in English for easier understanding. Mr. Griggs bought a blue Volkswagen Beetle car for Guruji to travel around on his mission in Trinidad. When it was evident that Guruji would be in Guyana for a indefinite period, the car was sold and Mr. Griggs bought a similar car with the same blue colour for Guruji to use in Guyana.

Mr. Griggs had retired from his executive employment in the oil industry in Trinidad. He was highly respected in the oil industry and his community. He made generous undisclosed donations to Guruji in Trinidad and in Guyana. I suspect some of his contributions were meant for the building of a house in the Ashram for Guruji. He was genuinely upset when he saw that Guruji was living in a humble shed.

Mr. Griggs and his son, Ancil, were invited by Guruji to spend some time in the Guyana Ashram. Mr. Griggs spent most of his time doing jap or meditation sitting on the floor of the temple. He frequently fasted and his diet was often crushed nuts and honey. He ate the same food prepared for Ashram residents. He was proud to wear his Mala (rosary) around his neck. He learned a lot from Guruji in Trinidad and practiced the Hindu way of life.

He was a happy and smiling man who enjoyed the company of the Brahmcharies and other Ashram residents. He was a short, bulkily built and balding gentleman about sixty-five years old. He dressed in short sleeves shirt and knee length trousers. He wore open rubber or leather slippers. He spent a lot of time in the evening chatting with Guruji. His sleeping accommodation was in the Dormitory. Guruji ensured that his time spent in the Ashram was comfortable and pleasant. After a Sunday morning Havan service and Artie, Guruji introduced him to the congregation and praised his contribution and dedication.

After a few months, Mr. Griggs returned to Trinidad leaving Ancil behind. We assumed that Mr. Griggs was hoping that Ancil would become the first black Brahmcharie. Ancil was a likeable boy about fourteen years old. He was full of fun and mischief, but worked hard and helped out with Ashram chores willingly. His particular responsibility was to look after 'Gladys', the Ashram milking cow. Guruji had purchased the cow from a devotee to provide milk for a sick Brahmcharie and the Ashram. Ancil milked the cow, cleaned out its pen and provided the evening fodder. Once, Ancil was digging trenches with other workers and Brahmcharies, when he suddenly yelled out' I cut my foot with the shovel'. We were aware of his boyish pranks and ignored him. He then deliberately hit his foot with the shovel and screamed very painfully. We all rushed to his aid. Although he had a slightly bruised toe, he laid on the ground and started to laugh heartily. Later, it became obvious that Ashram life was not his calling. Guruji then arranged for his return to his father in Trinidad.

As the Hindu College progressed steadily and successfully, Guruji embarked on building a Primary School in the Ashram grounds. The reasons were similar to the ones necessitated the start of the Hindu college. Additionally, younger Hindu children would have an associated affiliation with the Ashram, College, Hindu culture and religion. Hindu teachers did not have to convert to Christianity to teach in the Primary school. Female Hindu teachers could wear a sari or other Indian dress. Like the Hindu College, it would be non-sectarian and children of different religions would be given opportunity to learn and practice aspects of their faiths. The primary school would provide a feeder opportunity to the Hindu College. Guruji's long and persistent communication with Government Education Departments eventually succeeded in achieving approval and accreditation.

This was perhaps a first non-Christian denominational Government Primary School in Guyana and a very proud achievement for the Hindu community. Guruji employed paid contractors to build the Primary school. Brahmcharies were busy with teaching and other commitments. However, Mr. Doodnauth and Brahmcharies gave supplementary assistance at weekends. Brahmcharies Seecharan and Girija provided night securities (watchmen) duties by sleeping on or near the building materials with paraffin lamps. Guruji's occasional midnight patrol and conversation with us often offer comfort against the night elements. The Primary School was completed and opened in September 1957.

Although the Hindu College was gaining popularity, Guruji disliked stagnation and continued to work for further progress to enhance the profile of the College. He employed a young teacher, Mr. Rudolph Singh who was an outstanding student at Queen's College and highly recommended by the QC Principal, Mr. Sager Davis. Mr. Singh was a brilliant and confident young man with a good knowledge of tutorial sciences. He provided a stunning display of Science experiments during the opening ceremony of the Science Laboratory. Unfortunately, he was a very proud man and fully aware of his exceptional abilities, he found it difficult to work as a member of the teaching staff for the benefit of the students.

He had a personal altercation with Brahmcharie Suryaram, a very strong, determined and serious Brahmcharie who refused to be insulted and succumb to breaches of Ashram principles. Mr. Singh, in the presence of students, ordered Brahmcharie Suryaram to wash his plate from which he had eaten tined sardines. He threatened to report the Brahmcharie to Guruji if he refused his demand. A physical fight erupted and Mr. Singh was injured in the face and one eye. In anger, Brahmcharie Suryaram stormed away, packed his personal belongings and left the Ashram. This was regrettable, because we lost a dear brother who could have been a powerful servant of the Sangha. A few months later, Mr. Singh left the Hindu College.

SWAMI DIBYANANDAJI MAHARAJ

Guruji arranged for Swami Dibyanandaji Maharaj to come to Guyana from Calcutta and take over the role of Head of Science at the College. Swami Dibyanandaji was a reputable University Science Graduate and was directed by Sangha Headquarter in Calcutta to assist Guruji in Guyana. He was a relatively tall, slim and fair complexioned man perhaps in his late forties. He was quiet, unassuming and yet an effective communicator in the English language. All the Brahmcharies, Ashram residents and Sangha devotees liked him. At Sunday morning Havan ceremony, he played the harmonium and sung devotional songs, sometimes in the Bengali language. His version of 'Prabhu mishava shesha gunam' was heard for the first time in Guyana. It was deeply moving and devotional. He taught us to sing it as well, particularly to Brahmcharie Govind and myself.

Swami Dibyanandaji Maharaj

It was pleasing to hear him and Guruji communicating and chatting in Bengali. They spent many hours together talking about Bharat Sevashram actives in India and the work in Guyana. It was lovely to see Guruji laughing and enjoying their discussion. I saw Guruji in a similar hearty mood on two other occasions, once in Berbice, Guyana, with Professor Bhatacharya, Principal of Tagore High School, and the other with Mr. Dilip Basu in Stanlake Villas, London. In Public or privately, Swami Dibyanandaji always demonstrated utmost respect and obeisance to Guruji, his most senior Sangha monk.

Swami Dibyananda taught Chemistry and Physics to students preparing for GCE examinations. He worked hard and spent a great deal of time at night in the Laboratory preparing for forthcoming science tuition. He also assisted other Brahmcharies who were science teachers, particularly Brahmcharie Govind.

Regrettably, Swami Dibyanandaji was suffering from poor health. He became frail and weak, often unable to eat regular Ashram food. I was directed by Guruji to attend to his needs and particularly to prepare the type of food he liked and could tolerate. He also had difficulty coping with the different life styles in Guyana and missed the company of his brother monks in India.

Sadly, Swami Dibyanandaji died in March 1959. He was found lying on his back in a meditative position on the ground floor of the Primary school. I had just returned from Georgetown very early in the morning after attending Queen's College for lessons the previous evening, and was with Guruji who was reviewing my work in his house. A young Dormitory student excitedly reported that Swami Dibyanandaji was lying on the floor of the Primary school. I hurriedly rushed over to the school and found him as described. I feared for the worse and rushed back to inform Guruji. The confirmation of his death by our neighbour, Doctor Gillett, was obviously shocking and devastating to Guruji. The Brahmcharies, Ashram communities and supporters were saddened by his death. The body was removed to the upper floor of the Dormitory where people were able to observe a wake, pay their respects and mourn the loss of a valued and honourable Swamiji. On the 29th March 1959, Swami Dibyanandaji was cremated on the beaches by the sea across the boundary of the Ashram. A large crowd of people attended the cremation. When the ceremony was completed and the cremation fire subsided, Guruji sent us back to the Ashram. The devotees gradually drifted away. Guruji stood alone by the cremation spot for sometime. On the following morning we returned to the site to perform the last cremation rites. Guruji shouldered the heavy responsibility of the death of a Sangha monk.

MRS. SAHAWINE

Mrs. Mangri, an elderly lady popularly known as Mrs. Sahawine, generously donated her life savings and assets to Guruji. Her donation enabled Guruji to initiate several projects at the Cove and John Ashram and Sangha activities in London in particular and in North America. The most prominent was the Science Laboratory for the Hindu College. She had previously in 1955, donated money for the provision of piped water supply to the Ashram. Guruji used some of her donation to build an exclusive house in the Ashram grounds for her to reside in peace and comfort under the care and protection of the Ashram. The house was located on the western side of the College. It was self-contained with one bedroom, a living room and an ensuite bathroom with shower, washbasin and toilet facilities. A modern plumbing system was installed with drainage into a concrete 'cesspit' (cesspool) buried in the ground. This was the first type of construction and facility in the Ashram. Guruji insisted she should be as comfortable and secure as possible.

Mrs. Sahawine was a short, slim, frail and devout Hindu lady. She was quiet, unassuming and deeply religious. She was full of her faculties and was able to communicate and move about quite independently. She was careful with Hindu values of honour and respect. She often wore a white dress, skirt and top, and used a white shawl to cover her head. In her presence, one felt that she was always in a prayer mood. She would clasp her hands together and bowed her head when greeting anybody. In spite of her old age, she would sit on the floor with her legs fully extended out in front of her. She would then stretch out and hold her ankles with both hands and bend her head to touch her knees. She was proud to demonstrate this Yoga pose to Brahmcharie Seecharan and myself.

Guruji employed an elderly lady, Mrs. Dei, as a live in companion and to provide any necessary assistance for Mrs. Sahawine. Our cook, Mr. Foreman, provided and delivered all meals for her and Mrs. Dei. Brahmcharie Seecharan and myself were responsible for her care and welfare. Guruji and the Brahmcharies would individually and on separate occasions spend sometime chatting with her while she sat on the steps or platform of her house. She certainly enjoyed our time spent with her. At Guruji's request, female devotees of the Ashram, particularly Mrs. Jug Singh and Mrs. Dookram (Auntie Katie), attended to her personal needs and comfort as well as cleaning her house. Dr. Gillett was always at hand to provide medical care and attention.

Mrs Sahawine, accompanied by her carer, was a welcome presence in the Temple for Sunday morning Havan Service and Artie. She took her seat on the floor quietly and unobtrusively. Ashram devotees would engage in conversation with her after the ceremony, but being a shy and retiring person she would politely go back to her house.

Mr. Sahawine's health gradually declined and she eventually passed away quietly and peacefully. We were all saddened by her death. Everyone connected with the Ashram will forever be grateful for her contribution to the successes of the Ashram and Bharat Sevashram Sangha.

Although the focal points of Ashram activities were the continued successes of the Hindu College and Dormitory, other projects required attention. Guruji felt the need for security and safety of the Ashram. He embarked on a barbed wire fencing around the property from the bridge of the Ashram to the eastern embankment perimeter. The land was a neglected swamp and was previously used freely by local people to graze their cattle and sheep. When the land came under the ownership of the Ashram, the local farmers occasionally continued to herd their livestock onto the land. Fencing the area would keep away livestock and also add a measure of security to property and asset. As I had previous practical experience of this type of work, Guruji instructed me to complete this task with help from other Brahmcharies and voluntary workers.

Guruji agreed for a shop to be built to provide snacks and soft drinks for students from the Hindu College and Primary School. It was built and managed independently by supporters of the Ashram. This was the only unit in the complex in which Brahmcharies took no part in building. The shop was convenient and useful as there was no such facility for students in the immediate neighbourhood.

As there was no public supply of electricity in the district, Guruji invested in a large generator to provide electricity initially for the College, Dormitory and Temple. We built a corrugated zinc sheet housing with solid concrete base foundation for the generator as instructed by Guruji. Technical contractors installed the generator and the required wiring and light fittings. Brahmcharies learnt to operate, service and maintain the generator. Brahmcharie Jaikaran proudly assumed control for its effective use and maintenance. It was lovely to see the Ashram lit up at night. At 10.00 pm the generator was often switched off to save on fuel. We then reverted to paraffin lantern for further studies and other activities. I designed and built an elevated ramp to support heavy metal barrels of diesel fuel for the generator. Later other buildings in the Ashram were supplied with electricity from the same generator.

The Ashram land began to be separated into two sections. The North East area located the functional buildings of the College, Dormitory, Temple, Primary School, Guruji's house, Mrs. Sahawine's house, kitchen and other associated facilities. The South East section was still a barren land.

Guruji had this area cultivated with an effective drainage system and arranged for lots of coconut trees to be planted. The salty clay soil in this area proved difficult to grow vegetables. However, a small area near the Temple seemed to be fertile and as Guruji was always keen for the Ashram to be self sufficient, a small cottage garden started to flourish. Some devotees helped to plant some vegetables, particularly aubergine. Bumper crops were produced over a long harvest period and Ashram food consisted of aubergine cooked in a variety of dishes. Guruji occasionally can be seen watering and tending to the plants.

As the success, respectability and popularity of the Guyana Ashram continue to expand, Guruji was aware that the core principles of the Bharat Sevashram Sangha as laid down by Acharya Swami Pranavanandaji Maharaj should never be forgotten. These teachings are the foundation of the Ashram. Therefore the practice of poverty, begging, self-denial, obedience and the absence of pride and egoism must be practiced. Although these disciplines were implied and expressed in the hard physical and mental activities by Guruji's Brahmcharies, it was necessary to demonstrate them in other ways as well. The self-sufficiency programme of rice and vegetable farming, the collection and chopping of firewood for cooking, the cooking of communal Ashram food and washing of cooking utensils, the cleaning of toilets, the sweeping of classrooms and other areas were tasks undertaken by Brahmcharies. I remember a young girl student, the daughter of a constant devotee to Guruji, turned up for College early one morning and found me sweeping out her classroom. She immediately took the broom off my hands and continued the rest of sweeping. On many occasions, Guruji would be seen performing some of the above duties and picking up debris from the school perimeter. It was not unusual to see a Brahmcharie, who had just finished the last teaching period for the day, to be involved in these types of work.

A few Brahmcharies had no beds to sleep on. Brahmcharie Seecharan slept on the platform leading to the temple entrance and I slept on classroom desks or on the grass of the canal embankment in front of the College. It was necessary to demonstrate visible 'night watchman' or security for the Ashram to deter intruders and theft during major construction. Expensive building material, machinery and tools were tempting targets. Attempts were made to steal building timbers and flooring boards. Guruji would himself patrol the Ashram perimeter at night and occasionally ask us to walk and chat with him well after midnight. On rainy nights, Brahmcharie Seecharan and myself would sit on piles of building material and shelter under a tarpaulin sheet. These building materials were stacked together in a remote and vulnerable position. Once we chased away a potential thief who later reported us to the local police. He claimed we threatened to shoot him with a shotgun as he waded across the canal on to Ashram land and was confronted by Brahmcharie Seecharan and myself.

The formal academic education needs of the Brahmcharies were mentioned earlier. Although their spiritual development were inculcated in the physical and mental duties undertaken, they had to learn and practice other religious duties for the public as well as for their personal spiritual development. I shall relate a few structured training and guidance given by our Guruji.

Evening Artie was performed every day at 6.00PM in the Temple after which the Dormitory boys would bow down before the Alter of Guruji Maharaj and Guruji. They would then leave for their evening meal. The Brahmcharies would remain to read some of the letters Guruji Maharaj had written to his disciples and verses of the Bhagawat Gita as directed by Guruji. Guruji would then provide explanations and occasionally relate some aspects of the life and work of Guruji Maharaj. It was also a time to review the day's work and progress. The Brahmcharies would then bow down before Guruji Maharaj and Guruji before retiring for their evening meal. Guruji would be the last to leave the Temple.

Occasionally Guruji would summon one Brahmcharie to his home. Here Guruji would provide an opportunity for a one to one discussion and time for personal training and experience. Most Brahmcharies looked forward to this opportunity and I am sure, obtained immense spiritual benefit from this invaluable time spent with their Guruji.

Brahmcharies privately practiced their spiritual training of Jap, Meditation, Yoga exercises and Fasting. They read and studied Hindu religious texts, performed Sandya and Havan, played musical instruments and sang Bhajans. They were expected to read the Ramayan and Bhagawat Gita to the public and be effective public speaker. They had to respond to Ashram supporters who requested Havan services at their home. As in the case of academic education, the Brahmcharies achieved varied individual successes. Brahmcharies received sincere respect from the community in general. As they did with Guruji, devotees would welcome the Brahmcharies to their homes, immediately prepare a meal or refreshments for them and showed genuine pride and appreciation for their visit.

Some Brahmcharies fasted and went without sleep for a few days. Guruji insisted that we should not continue this discipline for longer periods because our teaching and hard physical duties could be affected. He advised there would be time for this practice at a later period.

The brotherly relationship of the first five Brahmcharies, mentioned earlier, was strong and constant. They worked, ate their meals, prayed, received training from Guruji and slept side by side, on the same floor. Each had his respective skills and abilities and was proud of and helpful with one another. There was never any disagreement, argument or jealousy. With Guruji at the helm, there was never any time or need for any discord among his disciples. In one of Guruji's discourses with us, I recall his reference to a letter of Guruji Maharaj written to his disciples about the need for brotherly love and support throughout the Sangha for its mission to be effective and successful.

During the early pioneering period of the Guyana Ashram, it was evident that observance of Hindu festivals, performance of Puja and Havan and reading of the Ramayan or the Bhagawat Gita were ceremonies rarely done at the Ashram. Priority was given to building and construction and the Brahmcharies training and discipline were relative to the work at hand. Dinesh Sukhi obtained an audio tape recording of Guruji's lecture at the opening ceremony of the new AshramTemple. In November 2014 on the occasion of Guruji's birth anniversary celebration at the London Sevashram Sangha, Dinesh played this recording for the audience. It was pleasing to hear Guruji's voice. In his speech, Guruji remarked that ceremonial worships and festivals were secondary to the dedicated and selfless work in Ashram life. A similar situation arose during the early days of establishing the London Sevashram Sangha. For the first four years there was never any public ceremony at the London Ashram. The one room occupied by Guruji and his Brahmcharies was not conducive to such ceremony.

OPPOSITION TO AND SUPPORT FOR GURUJI

Guruji received oppositions and threats from individuals and organizations. Two prominent Hindu organizations, which possibly felt threatened by Guruji, petitioned the Guyana Government to have Guruji deported back to India. Indirect personal threats and warnings were also issued to Guruji.

After the major ceremony for the opening of the Hindu College, Guruji chaired a public meeting at the Ashram to discuss his plans for the College, the Dormitory and future activities of the Guyana Ashram. In attendance were Hindu Pundits representatives, other prominent Hindu personalities and members of the local community. The meeting was well attended as Guruji outlined his plans. Later the meeting became disruptive by a few representatives who proposed a 'take over' of the management control of the Ashram by electing secular Chairman, secretary and treasurer. There was an obvious preconceived plan to get rid of Guruji. Later Guruji dissolved the meeting.

A carpenter contractor employed by Guruji to build a sluice opposite the College for the land drainage, almost physically assaulted Guruji during a loud argument about the way the work was done.

During the public riots in 1962, The Ashram and neighbouring districts were on high tension and unrest. The Ashram was vulnerable to attacks from rioters. Indirect threats to burn down the Hindu College were received. The local Police Inspector Mr. Jarvis, whose two sons were students at the College, was friendly and visibly supported

Guruji. He visited the Ashram and advised us on security and safety precautions. Swami Dibyanandaji, who had self-defense experience in India against riotous attacks on Hindus and Sangha Ashrams, gave us some basic training. Guruji was in London busily working to establish the London Ashram. Preparation to repel any attack was very thorough. Some of our defense strategy was made public to the students of the College hoping that information would reach potential troublemakers. On the Ashram side of the bridge over the canal, we made some strange markings with flowers and different coloured rice. We were hoping that a sense of mystery would deter intruders during the night. It worked. No attempt was made to cross the bridge during a night of serious riots and burning of properties in the district. However, on the following morning, college students were reluctant to cross the bridge. We hurriedly removed the flowers and rice and assured the students that it was safe to cross over the bridge.

After Mrs. Sahawine voluntarily donated her savings and assets to Guruji, her distant relatives continually threatened Guruji with legal actions for the donations to be given back to them. Although there was no legitimate claim, there was the anxiety of a possible personal attack on Guruji.

There were many other isolated individual disagreements, some from professed supporters of the Ashram. Guruji treated these problems as minor distractions and remained steadfast on his dedicated task. Guruji had experienced these type of set backs in India during his early days as a Brahmcharie and as a Swamiji. His fearless patience and determination was perhaps what endeared him to so many people from all walks of life. The personal threats and conspiracy appeared insignificant against the massive support and respect Guruji attracted.

I would like to mention some prominent people and leaders who frequently and voluntarily contributed to the successes of Guruji's pioneering work.

The Governor General of Guyana, Sir Patrick Renison, laid the corner stone of the Hindu College in 1956 and three years later opened the Science Laboratory. His speeches on both occasions were full of support and appreciation.

The Principal of Queen's College in Georgetown, Mr. Sanger Davis, was frequent visitor to the Ashram. He provided valuable advice and assistance to set up the Science Laboratory. He recommended and provided facilities for free tuition to Brahmcharie Teachers by his Graduate Masters from Queen's College.

Professor Bhatacharya, Principal of Tagore High School at No. 64 District in Berbice, communicated regularly with Guruji. Professor Bhatacharya was a Bengali scholar and an expert on the works of Tagore. He was contracted by the executives of the High School to manage the school for a number of years. He was well known for his composition in Hindi of a Guyana National Anthem. Guruji, a Bengali himself, enjoyed communicating with the Professor and Mrs. Bhatacharya in their native language. I was fortunate to accompany Guruji on one of his visits to their home in Berbice. Mrs. Bhatacharya cooked a special and delicious meal of no less than ten dishes for us. We visited the High School and I was given the honour of addressing the English Literature Class of students preparing for a public Examination.

Professor and Mrs. Bhatacharya were active in support of the local Hindu community and Mrs. Bhatacharya voluntarily conducted Indian cookery lessons.

Professor Sruti Khant, Principal of the Guyana Oriental College in Georgetown and Mr. Ramlochan, Principal of the New Amsterdam High School in Berbice , occasionally visited the Hindu College and provided welcome support to Guruji. Mr. Nowrang Persaud was at one time a Secondary School teacher at Mr Ramlochan High School and he also honoured me with the privilege of addressing his English Literature class. The assistance to Guruji from these educationalists was invaluable contribution to the successes of the Hindu College.

Pandit Usherbudh , a Vedic Sanscrit scholar and an eloquent speaker from India, arrived in Guyana by invitation from the Arya Samaj Hindu community. Shortly after his arrival, a Secondary School was opened in the neighbouring Mahaicony District with Pandit Usherbudh as Principal. Was this in response or a competition to Guruji's Hindu College? Eventually the School closed. However, Pandit Usherbudh continued to work with the Arya Samaj community and later became a frequent visitor to Guruji. I do believe he admired and supported Guruji's work. In 1964, Pandit Usherbudh was in London when I invited him as a guest speaker for the London Sevashram Sangha at the Maghi Purnima celebration of the birth anniversary of Sri Acharya Guruji Maharaj.

The Hindu Pandit community of Guyana eventually began to recognize and respect the pioneering work of Guruji. On many occasions, Guruji praised the work of the Pandits and publicly declared that their service was a major factor in the survival of Hinduism in Guyana and Trinidad. Pandit S Sharma and other Hindu leaders became regular advisor and supporter of Guruji.

The Muslim community highly respected Guruji and many Muslim individuals provided professional and manual assistance to the Cove and John Ashram and associated Milan Mandirs in Berbice. This was particularly evident in building and construction work. Guruji's relationship with the Christian community was equally respectful and successful. The Hindu College attracted students and teachers from different backgrounds and religious affiliations. Parents of the Muslim and Christian students were well known to Guruji who afforded them access and opportunity to discuss the progress of their children.

It gradually became evident that Guruji's principled work, as laid down by Acharya Guruji Maharaj, transcended sectarian and parochial values. It was inclusive of all religious affiliations for the purpose of a cohesive community. Later, Guruji's work at the London Sevashram Sangha demonstrated this principle more emphatically.

Dr. Cheddi Jagan, President of Guyana, and Mrs. Janet Jagan assisted Guruji in 1963 during a very difficult time, to obtain visas to the United Kingdom for his two Brahmcharies following an intervention from Lord Dowding in London. Lord Dowding was a friend and supporter of Guruji's work in London.

The assistance received by Guruji from famous and high profile personalities in Guyana is well documented. Their help and contribution will always be a legacy for the

Ashram and the Hindu community. It is also a testimony of trust, respect and praise for our Guruji.

SOME EARLY DEVOTED SUPPORTERS

It is also equally important to remember the contribution made by the ordinary men and women. Their unquestionable, tireless, constant hard work and sacrifice for Guruji was given because of the love and veneration they had for him. Their dedicated service was offered freely without reward or public recognition. Guruji's request for their assistance was treated with utmost priority, occasionally at some sacrifice to their family needs. These unsung devotees of Guruji were the 'salt' of the Ashram's earth. I agree with Brahmcharie Govind's recent remark to me that without these devoted people and the first five Brahmcharies, our Guruji would not have achieved so much success at the Cove and John Ashram which later became the springboard for Bharat Sevashram Sangha activities in other Western countries. I will try to recount the contribution made by some of these devotees of Guruji.

Mr. Doodnauth Sukhu was mentioned earlier in relation to the many building work at the Ashram. He was also active in support of Guruji's work outside the Ashram as well as working selflessly for other Hindu organizations in Guyana. Mr. Doodnauth and Mr. Beni Singh were passionate about the teaching of Hindi to children throughout Guyana. With the permission of Guruji, they were successful in introducing the teaching of Hindi in the Hindu College curriculum. They tactfully and respectfully taught Hindi to some Brahmcharies.

Mrs. Rookmin Doodnauth was equally dedicated to Guruji but always quietly and unobtrusively. Her love and sacrifices, particularly by allowing her husband to spend endless days at the Ashram, often extended to the Brahmcharies as well. Brahmcharie Govind and myself would enjoy her hospitality when we were stranded late at night in Georgetown without public transport back to Cove & John after evening tuition at Queen's College. On many occasions I found myself in this situation and turned up at her home in Camberville without warning for refuse. I am sure Guruji advised her to expect us occasionally. Once she provided a meal and offered me to sleep on a bunk bed from which she had thrown out her young children to sleep on the floor. I protested furiously, insisting that I did not sleep on a bed at the Ashram and I would be comfortable on the floor.

She refused to listen to my pleas and concluded that I was in her home and not the Ashram. She sat on the floor in front of me and watched me eating the food she carefully prepared. We chatted during the meal and like an elder sister, she insisted I had some more food. I accepted that such genuine kindness was demonstrated to me because I represented Guruji and the Ashram.

This devoted family experienced a most traumatic and sorrowful time at the illness and eventual demise of their son,Veda, who was only five years old. Guruji unreservedly supported and offered comfort to them during the difficult time. As requested by Guruji, Brahmcharie Govind and myself donated blood for the youngster as he was having frequent blood transfusion. When Deva passed away, Guruji, the Brahmcharies and dormitory boys spent the whole night at the Doodnauth's residence singing Bhajans and trying to console the family. Deva was the first child to be cremated in Guyana.

Mrs Dookram, affectionately known as Auntie Katie was another dedicated devotee. She was a quiet, shy and humble lady. She had boundless energy and dedication. She worked tirelessly for Guruji and the Ashram. She cleaned and scrubbed the floors of the Temple, the Dormitory, Guruji's house and Mrs. Sahawine's house. She started working soon after the Temple ceremony on Sunday mornings and finished late in the evening. She would then collect some clothing and other domestic material from the Ashram, take them home for washing and even ironing some of the garments and return them to the Ashram. Aunty Katie was the breadwinner of the family and worked very hard to maintain a respectable standard of living and provide education for her young family. She successfully cultivated vegetables and sold them for the family income. Her very best aubergine, pepper and pumpkin were reserved for the Ashram.

Mrs. Evelyn Jug Singh, like Mrs. Doodnauth was quietly an ardent supporter of Guruji. She was instrumental in introducing Auntie Katie to the Ashram. Mrs. Jug Singh organized a group of women, mainly from the Singh's families of Enmore district to provide assistance and voluntary domestic work for Guruji, the Brahmcharies, Mrs. Sahawine, the Temple and the Ashram in general. These dedicated ladies include Mrs. Champa Singh, wife of Mr. Seo Singh, Mrs. Harsadai Singh, mother of brother Beni Singh, Mrs. Roop Singh, Mrs. Budhoo, Mrs. Sharma and many other ladies of the district.

Mr. Jug (Jagajee) Singh was a stalwart of the Guyana Ashram. He provided regular assistance to Guruji advising him on effective contacts for financial support and donations. Mr. Jug Singh was well known and respected by the Hindu community in Guyana. His influence and presence at the Ashram was highly regarded by Guruji and the Brahmcharies. On many occasions he spent long hours in discussion with Guruji at Guruji's house and became a trusted confidant of Guruji. In times of difficulties, specific needs and his personal illness, Guruji sought the assistance of Mr. Jug Singh.

When Guruji was very ill and admitted in Georgetown Hospital, Mr. Jug Singh and his family together with few other devoted families provided regular care for his wellbeing and recovery. The Brahmcharies and Ashram residents were initially unaware of his sudden and serious illness. Guruji insisted that the work of his Brahmcharies and Ashram must be uninterrupted and unaffected by his illness.

A similar situation occurred in London in 1980 when Guruji was seriously ill and admitted to the Hammersmith Hospital in West London. The doctors, devotees and Guruji himself felt that he was unlikely to survive much longer than a few days. Guruji requested to see Mr. Jug Singh who was in Canada at the time. Mr. Jug Singh took an emergency flight to London. Mr. Lal Nawbatt and Mr. Jug Singh visited Guruji who was very pleased to see both of them. Guruji said to his doctor in the hospital ward that "Mr. Jug Singh is here now I can go home". However, we later learnt that Guruji instructed Mr. Jug Singh that a 1000 pounds donation to Guruji from a supporter for the publication of his book,

'Prophet of the new Hindu Age' must be returned to the donor in the event of his demise before the publication of the book. Mr. Jug Singh's brother Mr. Seo Singh and his family were also devoted supporter of Guruji.

Mr. Beni Singh, affectionately referred to as brother Beni, was also devoted to Guruji. In his own quiet and unnoticeable manner, he was passionate about Hinduism and voluntary social services to the Hindu community. Guruji consulted with brother Beni on the introduction of teaching Hindi in the College. Eventually, Hindi was included in the College curriculum and brother Beni occasionally helped out with Hindi classes. His support and dedication to Guruji continued in London from the early days of the London Ashram

He invited Guruji and his two Brahmcharies to his small one bedroom apartment in Earls Court, West London. He cooked a delicious meal for us on a one ring gas cooker, which when unused was stored under his bed in a cramped room. Brother Beni, like many Hindu students, experienced severe hardships in London at that time.

He nevertheless found time at weekends to serve the Hindu and local communities by voluntary social work of cleaning and decorating the homes of old and lonely people. I assisted him on a few occasions with this work.

Mr. and Mrs. Shastri Tiwari and their family were very devoted to Guruji. During 1962, Guruji stayed at their home in London for a period. When Guruji was ill in Hammersmith hospital in London, Mrs. Shastri visited and cared for Guruji almost every day. Many other concerned devotees also visited him in hospital.

During a major flood in Enmore, Guyana in 1964, many local people were displaced and relied heavily on voluntary help and donations. temporary accommodation was provided at the Cove and John Ashram for some people affected by the flood. Brother Beni organized a group of Guyanese families in London to collect clothing and monetary donations which were sent to assist with the relief work. On a personal note, I shall always be grateful for his kind assistance in Guyana and more particularly in London when I was in a desperate and desolate situation. Like Mr. Doodnauth and Mr. Jug Singh, brother Beni offered immeasurable and dedicated contribution to our Guruji and consequently, the eventual successes of the Bharat Sevashram Sangha activities in Guyana, Trinidad, London and North America.

Pandit S P Sharma of Kitty, Georgetown was a fervent supporter of Guruji and was a member of the original group of people who invited Guruji to Guyana. Pandit Sharma offered accommodation for Guruji at his home when he first arrived in Guyana and during the earlier weeks of his preaching and lecture tours. Brahmcharies Govind and Girija often enjoyed their hospitality and lodgings for a night on occasions when they were independently stranded in Georgetown after attending for private tuition in the evening. Guruji sought his advice on many matters, particularly on the immediate needs of the Guyana Hindu community. Pandit Sharma was a frequent visitor to the Ashram on special occasions as well as for a personal meeting with Guruji.

Mr. Budhoo, like Pandit Sharma, was a member of the group responsible for persuading Guruji to visit Guyana. Mr. Budhoo's residence was near the Ashram and his entire family was closely associated with Guruji and the Ashram.

Like Mr. Jug Singh, Mr. Budhoo was a regular confidant of Guruji. Almost every New Years day, he entertained Guruji, the Brahmcharies and the Dormitory students with an elaborate meal at his residence. When Mr. Budhoo died, Guruji and the Ashram were at hand to provide spiritual support to the family. Guruji lead the funeral procession for his cremation.

The Berbice Hindu community, mainly from the districts of Albion, Port Mouurant, Nigg and Canji was equally devoted to Guruji. The very early regular supporters were the Doobays, Dalgeets, Keso Rams, Auntie Sardarin and family, Matadins, Ramayas, Basdeos and many more families. Mr. Ramdhani Bahadur and Mr. Biss Ragubeer of Canji district were prominent personalities of the Canji Hindu Temple. I am grateful to these two gentlemen as they were responsible for my first meeting with Guruji . They were active workers for the local Hindu community and were closely connected with the work of the Bharat Sevashram Sangha since the visit of Swami Advaitanandaji and his preaching group in September 1951. Their relationship with our Guruji grew rapidly. Along with other devotees of Berbice, they made frequent trips to the Cove and John Ashram. Shiv Ratri celebration at the Ashram was considered as a pilgrimage for the Berbician Sangha devotees.

There were many unnamed supporters and anonymous donors who recognized and respected Guruji for his pioneering and missionary work. They varied from a humble bus or taxi driver who would decline fees for their service to a wealthy and generous person donating large sums of money.

Occasionally, Guruji would be vehemently angry when work progress was slow or with individuals or groups in the Ashram when there were breaches of Sangha principles. This brief outburst of anger often demonstrated the strong and powerful personality of Guruji evolved over years of Sangha Sanyasi discipline. It also reflected his dynamism on a different spiritual plain.

However, his love for his Brahmcharies, disciples and devotees was unconditional. He cared for their health, welfare, domestic and social needs. He personally bought oranges, apples and other fruits for the Brahmcharies and dormitory students. He ensured there were three meals daily for all Ashram inmates. Occasionally I accompanied Guruji in his car to travel to Georgetown to purchase groceries for the Ashram. After a public Gita Yagna at the Ashram, Guruji instructed the Brahmcharies and Dormitory students to sit on rows of College benches and desks in front of the Temple. In view of a large crowd of people who had attended the ceremony, Guruji personally served us food smiling and joking all the time. He remarked that we must eat heartily as we appeared thin and gaunt and the public should not feel his Brahmcharies were starving. Visitors arriving at the Ashram at any time during the day or night, after a cordial welcome would be offered Ashram food (Prasad), even if his Brahmcharies had to hurriedly prepare a meal. This was a regular Ashram duty as instructed by Guruji and carried out at the Guyana and London Ashrams, at least during the life and service of Guruji.

Guruji bought a refrigerator for the Brahmcharies and Dormitory students, while he used a large earthen goblet with stones in it to keep his drinking water relatively cool.

The secular teachers employed by Guruji were paid a salary. The teaching duties of Brahmcharie teachers were voluntary and unpaid. However, Guruji would give each Brahmcharie a small nominal sum of money to obtain items of personal needs. Few Brahmcharies declined the offer, but Guruji insisted they should accept it.

He ensured that his hard working Brahmcharies had adequate food and necessary rest. I recall a minor accident when I fell through the upper floor timber joists while working on the building of Guruji's house. I injured my head slightly and incurred a mild concussion. Guruji insisted, much to my protest, that I should go and lie down because I showed possible signs of shock and exhaustion.

Guruji was aware that some of his Brahmcharies worked and studied late into the night. Regular Ashram and teaching duties often lasted up to midnight. This meant that personal studies, particularly in preparing for public examinations, started after midnight and went on to 4.00 am and possibly much later. Occasionally, Guruji would leave his house, walk quietly up the stairs of the Dormitory at 3.00 am and caringly advise one to go to bed. As examination time was approaching I found I had to study much harder. I secretly had to take tablets to stay awake and survive on only a few hours of sleep. After I completed my public examinations, I stopped taking the drugs but could not resume normal sleeping patterns. Guruji found out what I had done. As a concerned and loving father, gave me a mild telling off and rushed me off to see Dr. Gillett.

Although very careful and thrifty with Ashram funds, Guruji spared no expenses for our medical, optical or dental care and attention. Brahmcharie Govind was not always in the best of health. He felt that Guruji bought the milking cow 'Gladys' so that he could supplement Ashram's diet with fresh milk. Similar care was expressed to Swami Dibyanandaji who also had health problems. Guruji was so loving and proud of his Brahmcharies that he informed the senior Holy Fathers of the Sangha Headquarters in Calcutta about their work and spiritual progress. Swami Advaitanandaji Maharaj wrote letters with blessings and encouragement to a few Brahmcharies.

As the Guyana Ashram and Hindu College continued to progress successfully, Guruji ventured into starting a Sangha Ashram in London.

****

LONDON SEVASHRAM SANGHA -17 STANLAKE VILLAS. GURUJI'S PIONEER WORK BETWEEN 1961 AND 1967

In the late summer of 1961, London saw a 'strange man clothed in a simple saffron robe and a pair of cheap rubber sandals' as described by the Guyana chronicle newspaper. He was our Guruji, Srimat Swami Purnanandaji Maharaj on a stop over visit on his journey from Trinidad to India. He immediately saw the needs of the Hindu community in London and the possibility of spreading invigorated Hinduism under the auspices of the Bharat Sevashram Sangha to the elite of London and perhaps further into Europe.

Hindus, mainly Sangha devotees and students from Guyana and Trinidad, greeted Guruji and later supported him in his efforts to establish a Sangha centre in London. He first resided in an apartment in Onslow Gardens, West Kensington, London. In the winter of 1961, Mr. Dilip Basu, a Bengali student from Kolkata, India, first met Guruji in a local post office. He bowed down and touched his feet with respect without knowing anything about Guruji. Mr. Basu recently remarked that it was the most memorable and influential meeting in his life. He and his family continued to support Guruji and the work of the Bharat Sevashram Sangha.

From his apartment in Onslow Gardens, Guruji conducted meetings and discussions on Hinduism largely to a European audience. He gave lectures at colleges and universities on aspects of Hinduism and the Bhagwat Gita. London intellectuals from prominent institutions and universities became very interested in Guruji's lectures. Particular interest was demonstrated on his references to and interactions with different religious groups. Three prominent and influential personalities were very supportive to Guruji and his work in London. They were Lord Downing, Air Chief Marshal during World War 2, Lord Sorensen MP and later member of the House of Lords, and Lady Ravensdale of Kedlesdon, daughter of Lord Curson.

Later, Guruji moved from his apartment in Onslow Gardens and stayed at the residence of Mr. Jogeshwar in Kentish Town, London. Mr. Jogeshwar and his family were great supporters of Guruji's work in Trinidad. Mr. Harry Persaud and Mr. Dindyal also Trinidadians, were very happy to see Guruji in London. They were Sangha devotees in Trinidad. While still a young boy, Mr. Harry Persaud was initiated by Swami Advitanandaji Maharaj in Trinidad in the early 1950's. These three gentlemen were among other Hindus from Guyana and Trinidad who arranged for the performance of Pujas and Havan and also readings of the Ramayan and Bhagavat Gita by Guruji at the homes of devotees in London. Guyanese support for Guruji's work in the early days was predominantly from Mr. Beni Singh and Mr. and Mrs Shastri Tiwari.

There were two other situations that influenced Guruji's decision to start a branch of the Sangha in London. In the early nineteen sixties, Hindus in London along with other non-white foreigners, experienced open racial discrimination. Advertisement for rented accommodation often read 'no blacks and no dogs'. Foreign students studying at London Colleges and Universities faced particularly hardships.

It was also difficult to obtain vegetarian food at student hostels, colleges, universities, public cafes or restaurants. Mr. Basu once ordered baked beans on toast in a café. When the meal was served, he discovered that bits of fried bacon and eggs were on the baked beans.

Their isolation from Hindu religious, cultural and social interactions also added to their dilemma. There were Hindu organizations, cultural activities and small temple gatherings in rented halls or recreation centers. However, these were often parochial with ceremonies and social communications being conducted in different Indian languages and dialect. London Sevashram Sangha would provide an inclusive and effective atmosphere particularly for students and families from Guyana, Trinidad and India. Guruji also had the idea that as the Sangha progressed, agreeable accommodation could be provided for students possibly like the dormitory at the Hindu college in Cove and John, Guyana.

Guruji must have felt that it was the wish and blessing of Guru Maharaj, that a branch of the Bharat Sevashram Sangha should be established in London. This was then the birth of the London Sevashram Sangha. In January 1962, Guruji purchased the property at 17 Stanlake Villas, Shepherds Bush, London W12. It is worthwhile to note here that in January 1952, the Sangha Cultural Mission to Trinidad and Guyana under the leadership of Swami Advaitanandaji Maharaj, was returning to India 'via London where the Mission worked for a short time'. This was recorded in the Sangha Report on Activities between 1950 and 1952 by the then General Secretary Swami Vedanandaji Maharaj. Perhaps the spiritual seed of the Bharat Sevashram Sangha was first sown at this time only for our Guruji to fertilize and nurture it ten years later into the London Sevashram Sangha.

The property at 17 Stanlake Villas, Shepherds Bush.

The challenge for Guruji was massive with problems and demands vastly different from what he experienced in Guyana and Trinidad. The most apparent was financial and profiling of the Sangha. He was to undergo severe hardships and sacrifices.

The property consisted of a basement with two rooms and a kitchen; the first floor with two rooms, a bathroom and toilet; the second floor with two rooms and a small kitchen; the third floor with one large room, a box room with cooking facilities outside the rooms. With the exception of one room on the ground floor, all other rooms were rented out to paying tenants. Part of the purchase agreement was that the resident tenants should continue with their tenancy until they leave by mutual agreement. You will observe that there was only one bathroom and one toilet facility to be shared by ten residents. The income from the lettings helped with mortgage repayments and maintenance of the property. Guruji resided in and conducted his Sangha activities from the one vacant room on the first floor. The house was an end of terrace building with bedrooms adjoining. The other side of the property was partly adjoined to small industrial storage buildings. At the back, there was a small garden with a derelict greenhouse. The front view of the building was impressive. It was constructed with bricks of white stocks quality, large sash windows with concrete window sills, an imposing large and heavy front door as the main entrance from five wide stone steps leading to short path way and then to the pavement of the street.

It was situated in an oak and ash trees lined cul-de-sac with easy access to a main town road, public transport, shops and local market. It was a relatively quiet and eminently suitable location for the London Sevashram Sangha.

On the 5th March 1962, on the occasion of the birth anniversary (Maghi Purnima) of Guru Maharaj, Guruji celebrated the occasion at the assemble hall of the University Of London. The packed audience was made up of Europeans of different faiths, University students and Hindus from Trinidad, Guyana and India.The ceremony was chaired by Baroness Ravensdale. In her speech, she talked about the work of Guru Maharaj and praised Guruji for his efforts to extend His mission here in London.

The property at Stanlake Villas was purchased comparatively cheaper than expected for the location, but with a very high interest rate on mortgage repayments. Although structurally sound, it needed extensive internal repair work and upgrading of amenities and facilities for the purpose of conducting Sangha work. Guruji needed immediate and active assistance. He therefore arranged for myself and Brahachari Binode, now Swami Nirlapnandaji, to come over from Guyana to London. We experienced frustrating problems in trying to obtain visas to London. Guruji managed to secure an intervention from Lord Dowding who wrote to the British Embassy in Guyana and Dr. Cheddi Jagan to facilitate the required visas. Later, Mrs. Janet Jagan invited us to a meeting with her and visas were subsequently issued.

Securing the cheapest fare, we traveled by a single engine plane, possibly used to transport small animals, to Trinidad and then by ship, the 'Ascania,' arriving in Southampton, England in August 1963. We then traveled by train to London. After a long and trying overall journey, we were pleased to see Guruji at Waterloo train station in London. We had not seen him for over eighteen months. We bowed down and touched his feet in reverence and respect. Guruji was genuinely happy to see us and greeted us with a gentle embrace. Guruji was with two English supporters, Mrs. Richards and a gentleman whose name escapes me. They drove us in their car from Waterloo station to Stanlake Villas.

First impression of London was disappointing. The weather was cold and foggy and everything seemed dull and dirty. I suppose this was expected as we had just arrived from a very hot climate in Guyana where everything was bright and colourful.

Accommodation for Guriji, Brahmchari Binode and myself was a single ground floor room measuring approximately fourteen feet by twelve feet with a high nine feet ceiling. There was one entrance door and very large double sash window overlooking the small garden. The view was not entirely unpleasant looking at the back of neighbouring properties and their respective small gardens. The room was moderately decorated with sparse furniture of one table, one chair, one old wooden wardrobe and a large worn rug. Kitchen facilities comprised of a small gas two rings cooker, a small floor standing cupboard and small butler sink. These were located in one corner of the room near the window. On the adjacent corner of the same wall, we later built an altar for Guru Maharaj with a curtain screen. There was no bed.

The sacrifices and suffering Guruji endured in London were perhaps greater than what he experienced in Guyana during the early days of building the Hindu College. As we had often seen in many aspects of his life and work, Guruji continually demonstrated how he was a great and unique Sangha sanyasi.

In this single room, Guruji and his two disciples conducted Sangha activities, cooked ate, slept and performed respective spiritual disciplines like prayer, meditation and Arti to Guruji Maharaj in the mornings and evenings. We slept on the floor covered with an old threadbare carpet. Sometimes during the night while we were asleep mice gnawed away at the soles of our feet. To facilitate some measure of privacy for Guruji, we moved the old wardrobe to one corner of the room allowing for enough sleeping space. We shared one bathroom consisting of one toilet, a washbasin and a hipbath with nine other people in the building. Occasionally we used the facilities of the local public baths.

Winter presented particular problems. There was no central heating system. Every resident used paraffin heaters for heating. We relied on donated used winter clothing and blankets. The soot from paraffin heaters can be seen floating in the room. The window had to be opened to dispel the soot and obtain some fresh air. We often welcomed the opportunity to visit public libraries or the reading room of the British Museum for research and preparation for lectures. We received a temporary respite from the cold at these public places. Except for the occasional seasonal flu and a bout of chicken pox suffered by Brahmchari Binode and myself, Guru Maharaj kept us well and healthy.

In the earlier days, there was very limited contact with many Hindus in the area because every effort was concentrated on the construction work and establishing the Sangha on a solid foundation. The immediate task was the renovation and construction of additional facilities for effective Sangha activities. Guruji had already obtained local planning and building permission to go ahead with construction of a two-floor extension at the back of the property and also a side extension of the second and third floor. The new construction work would provide each floor as a self-contained apartment with kitchen and bathroom facilities. Two additional rooms, one at basement level and above, another room at first floor level, would enhance the property considerably.

The cost for all this work was extensive and would have been impossible if we had to pay contractors to complete the work. We had to do the construction and all associated work like carpentry, plumbing, electrical, rendering, plastering and decorating. The courage and resourcefulness of Guruji had been immeasurable. As he had so often done, particularly in Guyana and Trinidad, Guruji undertook tremendous risks with fortitude and strong determination to create yet another tangible miracle. These two words 'fortitude and strong determination' are exact words of Guruji Maharaj to Guruji personally at the time when Guruji first decided to join the Sangha. I have written about this incident later in the chapter on the early life of Guruji in India. Reflections confirmed that the blessings of Guruji Maharaj were with us throughout this almost impossible struggle.

Guruji enrolled us at a college to learn about British Building constructions laws and the theoretical and practical aspects of bricklaying, plumbing, carpentry, plastering, electrical work and decorations. In addition to theoretical studies, we also had to be successful on the practical work. Brahmchari Binode studied electrical work. I had to learn the other requirements up to 'City and Guilds' standards and take the required examinations.

Within six months, we achieved sufficient qualifications and skills to start the construction. We were lucky to have an immediate neighbour at Stanlake Villas who was a one-man general builder, plumber and decorater. Occasionally when time permitted, I would go out and work with Mr. Mike Andrusko, a Polish Catholic gentleman, to gain valuable practical experience. Mr. Andrusko once had a contract to build a small kitchen extension. He was inexperienced on bricklaying work and asked me to help him with the construction of the foundation and outer shell brick walls. He later made a generous monetary donation for my assistance. Both Mike and Eve Andrusko were very kind and supportive to us. I can still remember cups of tea or coffee being handed to us over the shared garden wall. Eventually, the required construction work began.

Brahmchari Binode and myself worked like people possessed to complete the task. In Guyana and in Trinidad, devotees and supporters of the Sangha often provided help with manual work. Here in London, there was no such help available. This was understandable as people had full and varied commitments with very little spare time to provide assistance. Credit is however due to Mr. Sonny Singh, a young Trinidadian, who had rented a small room on the third floor of the property. Whenever time allowed from commitments at college and work he would offer some help. When we first arrived at Stanlake Villas, Mr. Singh prepared a meal for us.

In1963, building tools and materials were basic with no mechanical or electrical equipment so prevalent today. Concrete mixing was done manually. Heavy cast iron soil pipes were the legal requirements for sanitary plumbing. Demolition work was done by use of heavy sledgehammers, steel bolsters and chisels. Moving of all building material from the public road was done manually up a flight of stairs to the front door, through a corridor then down a makeshift stairs to the building site. Building work on the second and third floors required carrying similar materials including very heavy reinforced steel and concrete lintels up six flight of stairs.

Extension work at Stanlake Villas London Ashram, 1965

Building regulations at the time required a foundation dept of six feet and three feet wide on an area fifteen feet by twenty feet. The foundation trench was dug out using pick axe and shovel. Once the building surveyor was happy with the trench, it was filled in with base concrete foundation three feet wide and two feet high. The new foundation had to be skillfully butted under the foundation of the existing property. This major work had to be done in one attempt without any overnight break. Cubic yards of ballast had to be manually mixed into foundation concrete on the street, fetched in buckets through the house and compacted into the foundation trench. This work took a full day and late into the night before it was completed by two Brahmcharies and their Guruji.

This kind of determination and dedication was reminiscence of similar work undertaken and inspired by Guruji in Guyana. A building foundation work was in progress with several people helping with different activities. Devotees and helpers could provide assistance only up to midnight. People began to drift away as they had their respective work commitments on the following day. Around 01.00 hours, Guruji sent some Brahmcharies and resident students to get some sleep and to be ready for College activities in the morning. It was apparent that the overall concreting work had to be completed for effective foundation strength. Guruji, Brahmchari Seecharan and myself continued with mixing concrete and pouring it into the foundation trench. Eventually, Guruji instructed Brahmchari Seecharan, later Swami Vidyanandaji, to go and get some rest as the major part of the work was near completion. It was difficult to watch Guruji pushing a wheelbarrow full of mixed concrete and smilingly supportive to us at the same time. The final stages of spreading, compacting and aerating the concrete foundation lasted until 04.30 hours before Guruji and myself retired from the work place. This was one of those rare occasions when you felt privileged to have a one to one interaction with our great Guruji.

At Stanlake Villas, work then started on the erection of the nine inches bonded brick walls for the two floors up to and partially above roof level. Eventually the construction was completed with two types of flooring, one concrete and one wooden, two ceilings and the roof. Internal concrete rendering and plastering of walls and ceiling, carpentry work on doors and windows electrical work and plumbing were all associated requirements and were completed in compliance with required building regulations.

Similar type of work was undertaken for the second and third floors extension. Additionally, new plumbing had to be done to provide facilities for toilets and gas cookers. Working at a height of over forty feet without external scaffolding and leaning over a wall to lay bricks was precariously dangerous. Throughout this frantic work commitment, Guruji's caring and loving support was boundless. On several occasions he cooked and served us meals and insisted we had adequate rest. Whenever he could, he worked with us and fetched buckets of bricks and concrete. His smiling face and occasional jokes, his paternal concern for our welfare and a sense of pride of what was being achieved gave us strength and encouragement. It was also the Grace and Blessing of Shree Guruji Maharaj that helped us with the endeavor.

While this extensive building work was being carried out at Stanlake Villas, other Sangha activities had to be addressed. After a full day of manual work, evening arti and a meal, we concentrated on the publication of the London Sangha magazine, 'Hinduism'. Guruji started this monthly magazine to publish the varied aspects, philosophy and teachings of Hinduism as he had generated a great deal of interest through his lectures to the Western world. Guruji felt that this periodical would also help to promote the work of the Bharat Sevashram Sangha and the life and teachings of Guruji Maharaj. This idea finally culminated in the publication in 1985 of the book 'Prophet of a New Hindu Age' by Guruji and professor Ninian Smart.

The magazine was in the form of a booklet measuring five and half inches by eight and a half inches with saffron coloured outer cover and boldly emblazoned 'Hinduism'. It was first circulated to known academics, intellectuals and leaders of religious organizations. Copies were sent to Universities, colleges, libraries and the reading room of the British Museum. Some copies found their way to Germany, Poland and Czechoslovakia. The Hindu community associated with the Sangha in London, Guyana, Trinidad and India also benefited from this periodical. It was therefore obvious that the profiling structure of the periodical and the quality of articles and material published should be of a high standard to be effective. This meant a lot of hard and dedicated work. Guruji enrolled me at a college, yet again, this time to study basic skills in journalism. I also had private lessons from a popular journalist who provided some valuable recommendations for the layout of the magazine. Miss Claire James provided me with an opportunity to address a college audience followed by a debate on 'Reincarnation'. She seemed pleased at the outcome of the exercise and provided a positive feedback. Guruji invited appropriate articles from many sources. He wrote several papers himself and obtained contributions from his Sangha brothers and eminent personalities in India. The contents were generally on Hinduism and Hindu philosophy written as articles, lectures, letters, poems and prayers. Dr. Dusan Kafka, a Vedanta student from Prague, was a regular contributor. Then followed the associated task of reviewing articles, proof reading and correction for final publication and circulation.

Guruji had to respond to many requests for us to lecture at seminars and meetings in London and other locations in England particularly at Canterbury in Kent, Norwich in Suffolk and Guildford in Surrey. The World Congress of Faiths frequently requested Guruji to address their conferences and meetings. Research and preparation for those obligations often proved exhaustive and time consuming. While dealing with our college studies and domestic chores, we tried to help Guruji with local and foreign communications. Guruji also had the overall management of the Guyana and Trinidad Ashrams. In the early sixties there were no computer, email or digital communication facilities. Most of the written work was done by the use of an old and beaten up Remington typewriter.

THE WORLD CONGRESS OF FAITHS

In 1936 Sir Francis Younghusband founded The World Congress of Faiths 0rganization. Sir Francis was born in India in 1863 and was later an Army Officer in the British Army in India. He was greatly influenced by Hinduism and Hindu culture. He was a student of comparative religions and was convinced that there were common beliefs in all major world religions. After a series of successful Inter Faiths conferences, Sir Francis established the WCF organization. Here in London, Lord Dowding was President and Lord Sorensen was Chairman of the WCF during the early sixties. Lady Ravensdale often substituted the chairmanship at some of WCF conferences. Guruji was the only representative of Hinduism and his contribution through lectures and involvement was highly appreciated by this august organization. In June 1964, Guruji was a member of the WCF Executive Council.

SOME OTHER ASHRAM ACTIVITIES

The following is a brief diary of some additional activities undertaken:

1. January 7th 1962. One of the many lectures given by Guruji, at WCF meetings.
2. March 5th 1962. Maghi Purnima Celebration at the Assembly Hall of the University of London. The event was chaired by Lady Ravensdale with presentation by Guruji on the Life and teachings of Guru Maharaj.

3. February 8th 1963. Maghi Purnima Celebration at the London University Assembly Hall. Lord Dowding presided over a large audience and announced the formal opening of the London Sevashram Sangha.
4. October 27th 1964. An address to Students and invited guests at the Bromley Technical College.

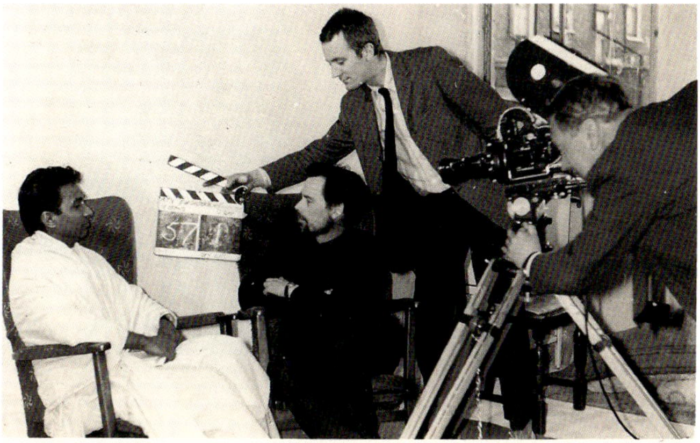

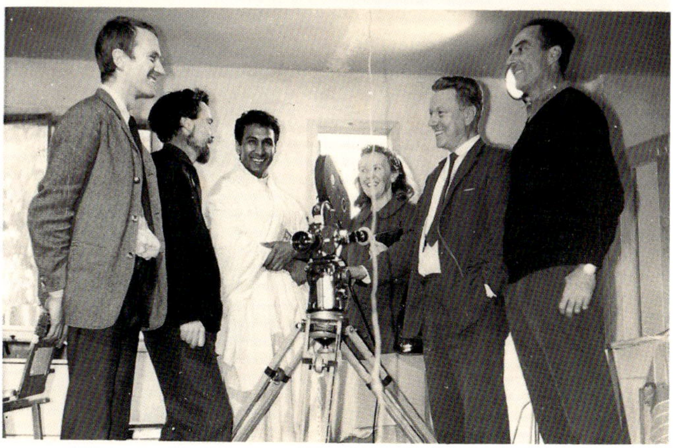

5. The British Broadcasting Corporation (BBC) conducted and filmed an interview at the Stanlake Villas Ashram on Sangha activities in London as part of a documentary on Eastern Religions.

6. March 15th 1965. A speech on Hinduism to the Women's Institute of the Parish Church of St. Paul. Lord Sorensen was guest speaker. We were invited on two further occasions to speak.

7. June 1965. We were invited to a reception at the Indian High Commission's Office in London to meet Mr. Lal Bahadur Shastri, the Indian Prime Minister.

8. December 19th 1965. As requested, we gave a lecture on Re-incarnation to the members of the influential London Rotarian club. This was followed by a lively and interesting discussion. There were several similar appearances as guest speakers at colleges, clubs, churches and at the Shah Jeehan Mosque in Woking, Surrey. The experience of speaking about Hinduism to a largely Christian audience at the Norwich Cathedral was overwhelming.

9. On the 6th February 1966 we celebrated Maghi Purnima at St. Michael's Hall in Golders Green, London.

The ceremony was chaired by Lord Sorensen who praised Guruji for his pioneering work in London. Guruji was in Guyana at the time. We performed a Havan and arti ceremony followed by a talk on the life and teachings of Guruji Maharaj.

In 1964, Guruji was urgently needed in Guyana. We were left with instructions to complete the construction work, address the demands of the monthly magazine 'Hinduism' and substitute for him as a member of The World Congress of Faiths. In general we had to manage the needs of the London Sevashram Sangha effectively. Of course, Guruji provided constant advice and guidance from Guyana.

SUPPORT FROM BHARAT SEVASHRAM SANGHA HEADQUARTERS IN INDIA

We were further blessed with paternal support and guidance from senior Monks of the Bharat Sevashram Sangha in India. The holy Saintly fathers Swami Advaitanandaji Maharaj, Swami Akshayanandaji Maharaj, Swami Nirmalanandaji Maharaj and Swami Yatishwaranandaji Maharaj were among others who wrote to us periodically.

Their letters were, and in some measures are still, immensely inspirational. Particularly moving was Swami Advaitanandaji's letter asking me to go to India for 'darshan' from the blessed Senior Holy Fathers of The Bharat Sevashram Sangha. He also asked 'to dive deep in your heart and discover the highest Truth which lies dormant in you'. Understanding our 'difficulties' and struggle, Swamiji Maharaj further comforted 'I am sure our Merciful Lord is there to inspire and provide necessary strength and conviction to encounter these unfavourable circumstances. There is also a universal fact, that those who come out as the bearer of His Cross never meet with failure or disappointment'.

BY AIR MAIL
PAR AVION
हवाई पत्र
AEROGRAMME

Brahmachari Girija
Bharat Sevashram Sangha
17, Stanlake Villas
London, W.-12
England

SECOND FOLD
NO ENCLOSURES ALLOWED

SENDER'S NAME AND ADDRESS:
Swami Advaitanandji
Bharat Sevashram Sangha
Ahmedabad-9
India.

institution. We are glad to read that Swami Purnanand has been able to pick up a few more dedicated workers from B.C. Let us hope our work of reform and reclamation in those colonies will grow more and more with their help and assistance. You might have heard that one of the pillars of our organization His Holiness Swami Vijananandji, who was the Vice-President of our organisation passed away last year and the health of the few of the elders is also far from satisfactory. So you should try to come to India as early as possible, in order to have their darshan and blessings. Of course this depends upon the direction of your Guruji.

Lastly, I would advise you to pay greater attention to your inner progress and purification by exerting best for that. Try to dive deep in your heart and discover the highest Truth which lies dormant in you. May Lord give you peace and solace. I am very eager to send a copy of the new publication and shall send it soon.

Yours in the Lord.
A. Advaitanand

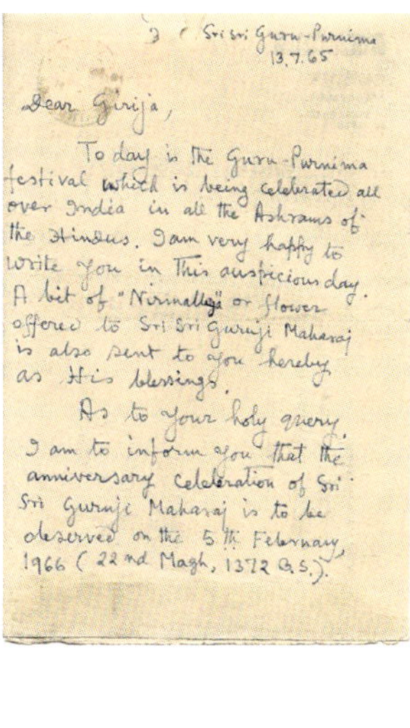

Sri Sri Guru-Purnima
13.7.65

Dear Girija,

To day is the Guru-Purnima festival which is being celebrated all over India in all the Ashrams of the Hindus. I am very happy to write you in this auspicious day. A bit of "Nirmallya" or flower offered to Sri Sri Guruji Maharaj is also sent to you hereby as His blessings.

As to your holy query, I am to inform you that the anniversary celebration of Sri Sri Guruji Maharaj is to be observed on the 5th February, 1966 (22nd Magh, 1372 B.S.).

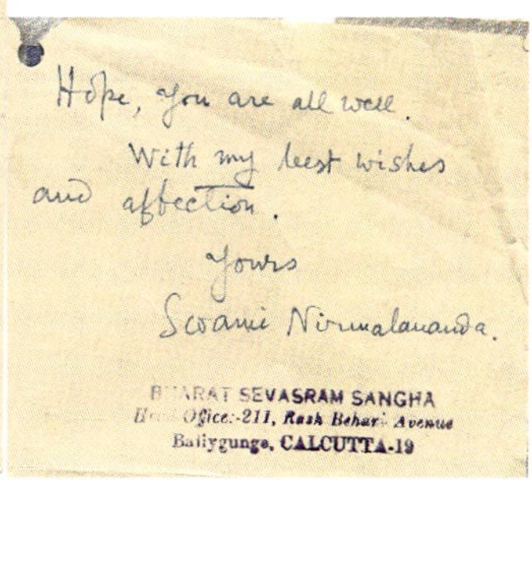

Hope, you are all well.

With my best wishes and affection.

Yours
Swami Nirmalananda.

BHARAT SEVASRAM SANGHA
Head Office:-211, Rash Behari Avenue
Ballygunge, CALCUTTA-19

In 1953, Swami Advaitanandaji Maharaj and his preaching party were conducting a Havan ceremony at a packed temple in Canje, Berbice, Guyana. The front door of the Temple was wide open and a crowd of people standing by the roadside could clearly see and perhaps follow the ceremony. I was a young boy and a member of that gathering, watching intently as Brahmchari Ramakrishnaji performed the Guru Arti. I was awe struck having never heard or seen anything so resounding and inspiring. I did not go into the temple and regrettably never met Swamiji Maharaj, but I still vividly retain the memory of the occasion. How strange it is that over ten years later, this holy and saintly Swamiji Maharaj would write to me with fatherly concern and spiritually moving words. I humbly accepted his guidance as the 'darshan' he referred to in his letter.

The initial deposited payment for the property at Stanlake Villas was made possible by the partial use of the funds donated by Mrs. Sahawine in Guyana. Everyone who knew Guruji will understand how careful and thrifty he was with Ashram monies. However, financial anxiety still weighed heavily on him particularly during the earlier years. In India, Guyana or Trinidad we would go out on the streets and beg for assistance and donation. In London, this was impractical and would have been ineffective. Brahachari Binode and myself occasionally did domestic chores, home cleaning and decorating for a small monetary remuneration. I often assisted our builder neighbour with building, plumbing and decorating work and would receive a generous donation. On one occasion working with Mr. Andrusko, I cleaned and repaired an overflowing septic tank. This was a very demanding and unpleasant task.

Guruji was reluctant to allow me to do this kind of work, but we needed every penny for the major expenses of building materials and publication of the journal. I would see the worry and sadness on his face. Once, I volunteered to take on a temporary job and even joked that I could make a lot of money from plumbing work. Guruji did not concede to this suggestion. By the Grace and Blessings of Guruji Maharaj we persevered with the struggle and survived intact. The construction work progressed slowly but successfully and eventually received the completion certificate from the Borough building Surveyor. The publication and distribution of the periodical 'Hinduism' also proved successful.

It would appear that the Hindu community did not feature a great deal during the early days of the Sangha because of the circumstances previously mentioned. However, when invited, we visited the homes of Sangha devotees and friends for meetings and performance of Havan ceremonies. Ricky and Bhaga Singh often welcomed us to their home in Holloway Road, London. At public meetings and celebrations of Hindu Holy festivals, particularly the Maghi Purnima celebrations, the London Hindu community provided dedicated support. One of Guruji's objectives to provide regular celebrations of Hindu festivals and Havan ceremony at 17 Stanlake Villas, was soon to be achieved as adequate facilities became available.

In August 1966, I was recalled to Guyana by Guruji to help with teaching and administration issues at the Hindu College. There was also a need for some construction work to build modern toilet and shower facilities for dormitory residents and college students. The College main building also needed repair and renovation work. With my building experience and skills achieved in London I was able to complete these required tasks before the 6th April 1967, when I returned to London and took my leave from the Organization.

This detailed, long and somewhat personal account of the early years of the London Sevashram Sangha is written with the hope that one will remember our Guruji as a truly great and unique Sanyasi of the Bharat Sevashram Sangha. He never wavered from the conviction that his life and work was dedicated to the wishes of Sri Guruji Maharaj.

In appreciation of our Guruji as a distinctly unique Sanyasi, I would like to refer to some significant incidents and achievements. The Western World was introduced to modern understanding and approach to Hinduism and its standing amongst other world Religions. Guruji's presentation skills and lectures on topical Hindu teachings and philosophy generated lasting interest with the elite and intellectual society of London. The monthly journal 'Hinduism' enhanced this growing interest and was perhaps the first of its kind in the Western World. It was the first time that Europeans became aware of the life and work of Sri Guruji Maharaj at the Maghi Purrnima celebrations mentioned before. Guruji later published his book "Prophet of a New Hindu Age" so that the Western World will become familiar with the Life and Work of Sri Guruji Maharaj.

Many prominent Hindu scholars and Swamis visited London and lectured on Hinduism, but these visits were often sporadic from itinerant exponents. Guruji's Sevashram Sangha in London would be a permanent base and focal point more accessible to everybody. In Guyana, a similar situation prevailed. Professor Sruti Kant, Principal of Guyana Orient

College in Georgetown, Professor Bhatacharya, Principal of Tagore High School in Berbice and Pandit Usherbudh were among Hindu scholars and leaders from India who provided commendable assistance to Guruji and the Hindu community in Guyana. Eventually they all left Guyana and returned to India. Guruji did not forsake his disciples and supporters in the Western World where he spent over thirty years of his life serving Hinduism and the Hindu community. It was ill health and the request of Sri Guruji Maharaj that prompted his retirement from his work in the Western World. He left London in January1986 on his final trip back to India. A few months later he departed from his mortal body on the 11th April 1986.

Swami Purnanandaji Maharaj demonstrated the highest qualities of a Sanyasi comparable with those of the holy ancient Vedic ascetics. Guruji lived a humble life and ate simple and basic food. He fasted on occasions when food was scarce or insufficient for his followers. He lived in huts and 'cow sheds' exposed to the elements of heat, wind and cold. He slept on the floor or on the ground. He shared his dwellings with mosquitoes, flooded water insects, rats and cockroaches. His personal possession was the humble saffron Sanyasi robe.

Perhaps a typical concept of a Sanyasi is one dressed in a saffron robe and sitting in deep meditation for long periods of time. His monastic life is spent living in a cave, a cell or a walled structure to protect him from the temptations of the secular world. He may also exile himself to a remote forest or the mountains of the Himalayas. A Bharat Sevashram Sangha monk however, is expected to maintain the discipline of a monastic life but dwell among and work for mankind. Guruji, like his brother Sangha monks, needed stronger determination and dedication to carry out the work of the Sangha.

While living as an ascetic, he interacted with the poor, the needy and people of prominence. He built Ashrams, colleges, temples and dharamsalas. He worked tirelessly for the poor and under privileged providing opportunities for formal and spiritual education. His disciples, devotees and supporters will now amount to thousands of people in the Western World. Their lives have been, and perhaps still are, greatly influenced by the legacy he left behind. Guruji's dynamism lives on.

Hindu Temple services were held in a small room, a recreation hall or a dedicated temple. Many Hindus attended for worship and celebration of Hindu festivals. Hindu priests or Pandits organized and officiated at these ceremonies. A Hindu community soon evolved with varying degrees of successes and effectiveness. Perhaps this is one of the reasons for the survival of Hinduism in the Western World. Guruji had often commended the Pandits for their contribution in this respect.

However, Guruji introduced the independence and responsibility of each Hindu to perform the Havan ceremony and other rituals without the intervention of another person. He gave us a sense of belonging and the confidence and opportunity to proudly declare 'I am or you are a Hindu'. His book the 'Hindutwam', the first of its kind in the West, supplemented his verbal teachings and practice. He encouraged us to perform Sandhya and Havan ceremonies at our homes with our families and friends without the need of a priest.

He suggested and helped to build a Hindu shrine or altar in our homes. He introduced total group participation of ceremonies at Sangha Centers for all without favour or exception. He introduced continuous singing of 'Hare Rama Hare Krishna' and 'OM Namah Shiva' for a twenty-four hours period with group participation on respective celebrations.

Other sections of Hindu Society now follow certain aspects of Guruji's pioneering work. There is also wide scale plagiarism of Guruji's Hindutwam prayer book. However, Guruji would be happy that his book, although plagiarized, was finding its way into the Hindu community at large.

Future Sangha Centers in the Western world, particularly in North America, will be the results and bear the hallmarks of Guruji's original struggle. At some of the Bharat Sevashram Sangha major Centers, particularly at Kalkota, Gaya and Puri, Guruji's photograph is among those of the first group of saintly disciples of Guruji Maharaj in temples specially erected to honour these Holy Fathers.

It is hoped that the legacy Guruji has left us will continue to progress and flourish while maintaining the principles and doctrines of the Bharat Sevashram Sangha. The life and work of our Guruji should never be forgotten. We have benefited so much and should be eternally grateful for his intervention in our lives. He was the light we needed to show us the way.

As 'the bearer of His Cross' Guruji stoically persevered with his mission here in London. The rigors of mental and physical discipline and particularly the isolation from his Sangha holy brothers in Kalkota, India, must have been difficult for him. During the occasion of Maghi Purnima celebrations, we saw the agony and sadness in his face as he missed sharing the pure, peaceful and exalting experience with the Sangha Holy Fathers in Kalkota.

I will conclude this chapter of the London Sevashram Sangha by relating some of my personal experiences as Guruji's disciple during this period. Living and working as he did in a lofty spiritual level of a saint, Guruji was also a person demonstrating acts of kindness, care, understanding, compassion, appreciation and fatherly love. A Guru and disciple relationship and experiences are impossible to describe accurately, either because of my inability to relate them or perhaps they are too precious to share. In Guyana and Trinidad, several disciples, devotees and supporters were closely associated with Guruji, but here in isolated London we had a one-to-one, or one-to-two interaction with him. It was therefore a privileged blessing for me to be so near to him in Stanlake Villas.

I cannot describe how we felt when Guruji cooked and served us food to our satisfaction before he himself could partake of any food or when he helped us with very hard physical work for long hours. We sat side by side in the Reading Room of the British Museum in Russell Square, London, researching relevant material for lectures and publication. We walked the streets of London, not behind him but as he insisted, side by side enjoying cheerful conversations. The occasional long walk from Russell Square to Shepherds Bush was equally satisfying. Guruji loved to walk. It was good exercise and saved money by ignoring public transport. Unlike in Guyana, the London Sevashram Sangha offered us the opportunity to work, eat, pray, perform Arti to Sri Guruji Maharaj standing shoulder to shoulder with your

Guruji and slept on the same floor every night. This cheerful and pleasant company with Guruji made one feel like a child having his dad all to himself.

On the night before Guruji left London to travel to Guyana, I found it difficult to sleep. I was restless and sorrowful at his departure in the morning. At 0300 hours, Guruji was aware of my sadness, and beckoned me to go to him. He embraced me and spoke softly and consolingly. I now realized that Guruji knew and I may have had a remote feeling, that this wonderful Guru and disciple relationship will not be repeated.

ADDITIONAL WORK BY GURUJI

At the suggestion of the publisher of this book and further requests from Guruji's disciples and supporters, I will try to relate some other achievements of Guruji as well as the astounding progress of Sangha activities in Western countries. I therefore apologize to readers if I repeat or refer to incidents already mentioned.

GUYANA

THE HINDU COLLEGE AND PRIMARY SCHOOL

The Hindu College and Primary school, extended and upgraded, made extensive progress in recognition and increased student numbers. In 1974, the Hindu College achieved second place in best results in public G.C.E and College of Preceptors examinations. A new library was built and science laboratory facilities and teaching of computer science were introduced. Many Hindu College students became teachers without having to change their religion. Female teachers were able to proudly wear saris or other Hindu outfits to work in both schools.

One gentleman, who wants to remain anonymous and currently living in England, was a Hindu College teacher. He proudly recalled his association with Guruji and the Brahmcharies. He supported Guruji in the London Ashram with devotion, dedication and many selfless services. He still provides generous assistance to Bharat Sevashram Sangha Ashrams and Swamis in many parts of the world in the treasured memory of our Guruji. Many other College students went on to become professional people in the Guyana Government departments. President Bharat Jagdeo was a Hindu College teacher and famous Guyana and International cricketer, Shivnarine Chanderpaul, was a Hindu College student. Guruji repeatedly advised that if Hindus really want to revive Hinduism, then they needed to be effectively educated to take their places as leaders in society and proud defenders of their religion.

INTERFAITH CONFERENCE.

In London, Guruji was actively involved in Interfaith Conferences and activities. As a committee member of The World Congress of Faiths, he lectured on Hinduism at many Religious Institutions including Churches, Cathedrals, Mosques, Buddhist Viharas and Sikh temples. In 1960, he organised and conducted a Guyana Interfaith Conference at the Ashram. It was successful and brought together leaders of different religions, including the Archbishop of Guyana. It complimented the fact that the Hindu College was a non-sectarian institute and students from both schools have facilities to conduct their respective religious prayers. Guruji emphasized and encouraged religious freedom for all.

CREMATION LAWS

After a long and persistent struggle, Guruji was successful in the reformation of Cremation Laws in Guyana. Cremation was indirectly prohibited or stopped. He had to convince the Health Minister, that it was the fundamental right of a Hindu to cremate a deceased. Moreover, cremation was cleaner and more hygienic than burial. A young son of Guruji's devotee was apparently the first child and Ashram devotee to be cremated. The second was Swami Dibyanandaji Maharaj. He was cremated on the beaches of the sea just across from the Ashram.

NEW MANDIR AT THE ASHRAM

In 1973, a new and larger temple replaced the previous temple structure. It provided increased facilities for the growing number of worshippers who turned up for various services and celebration of Hindu festivals. At the opening ceremony, Guruji made one of his impressively memorable speeches. He vehemently stressed the merits of dedicated selfless work full of 'Energy, Enthusiasm and Perseverance'. These are words of Sri Guruji Maharaj.

SHIV RATRI CELEBRATIONS

The Guyana Hindu Community often prepared extensively to attend this popular annual celebration at the Ashram. They traveled from all parts of Guyana particularly from the far reaches of Berbice and Essequibo for this twenty- four hours religious ceremony. In one year, it was estimated that over thirty thousand people converged on the Ashram for this holy celebrations.

THE MEDIATION PARK

The Ashram extended worship facilities on its grounds with many sections designated for specific individual or group worship. It offered a peaceful atmosphere where people can go for solitude, tranquility and solace. The Meditation Park supplemented the sanctity of the Ashram that I personally experienced in 1955 when I first joined the Ashram. This experience was described in the earlier part of this book. The park is accessible to people of all Faiths. In 1962 a lady of Chinese origin and a Buddhist, came to the Ashram and asked to spend the night in the Ashram for mediation and solace. Her family was in mourning at the loss of her mother and she wanted to offer her personal prayer. Brahmcharies provided evening refreshments and a secluded place for her mediation and rest for the night. In the morning she made a generous donation and expressed her gratitude.

GITA YAGNA FOR 365 DAYS

Guruji began to consider his work in Western countries was perhaps nearing the end. He then undertook one of his final major commitments. He conducted Gita Yagna from Berbice to Essequibo counties at villages and districts all along the long stretch of coastal regions of approximately one hundred and forty two miles. Services were also held on the islands of Leguan and Wakenham. This daily arduous work lasted for three hundred and sixty five days. It was perhaps a way of saying goodbye and offering his blessings to disciples and devotees. At his age and declining health, this was another monumental achievement. Brahmcharie Govind organized this undertaking. Mr. Doodnath and Mr. Budhoo provided devoted assistance to Guruji and Brahmcharie Govind. The above activities and many more were done amidst hugely political and social unrest in Guyana.

FURTHER PROJECTS.

After Guruji passed away, two additional projects were possible by the Guyana Ashram. These were proposed and sponsored by disciples of Guruji to honour his memory. A museum within the Ashram complex to exhibit the history of the Guyana Ashram was suggested. One devoted individual was keen to donate a sculptured bust of Guruji. Another devotee framed many photographs of Guruji and his work at considerable cost for display in the museum. The other project was the building of a branch of the Ashram in the Essequibo district. A large plot of land was donated and funds were available from enthusiastic devotees. Regrettably neither of these projects was taken up. Guruj's work ethics, dynamism, charisma, enthusiasm, single mindedness and persuasive personality were not there. It seemed the sparkle and drive of Sangha activities had so sadly stagnated.

GURUJI'S GUYANESE BRAHMCHARIES BECAME SANGHA SWAMIS.

Brahmcharie Seecharan to Swami Vidyanandaji in charge of Guyana and New York Ashrams.

Brahmcharie Vinode to Swami Nirliptanandaji in charge of London Ashram.

Brahmcharie Shivsankar to Swami Bhajanandaji in charge a Toronto Ashram.

Brahmcharie Bhaskar to Swami Shiveshwaranandaji in charge of New York Ashram.

Swami Vidyanandaji sadly died on the 28th October 2015.

Swami Shiveshwaranandaji took over responsibility for the New York Ashram.

Brahmcharie Vidur became Swami Shivsankar and took responsibility for the Guyana Ashram.

VISITING SWAMIS FROM INDIA.

Bharat Sevashram Sangha Monks are often delegated to different Sangha branches according to their skills and requirements. A number of itinerant and visiting Swamis from India came to assist or support Guruji periodically. Swami Dibyanandaji came to Guyana and headed the Science teaching in the Hindu College and Swami Brahmhanandaji was in charge of the Guyana Ashram and Principal of the Hindu College between 1967 and 1977.

TRINIDAD

When Guruji left Trinidad to work in Guyana, the Ashram was managed by Guruji's devoted followers with regular advice and support from Guruji. Later, Brahmcharie Shivsankar was sent to assist the devotees. Swami Dibyananadaji from India was for sometime in charge of the Sangha. Guruji made occasional visits to sustain confidence and encourage continued progress.

NORTH AMERICAN

The foundation of the Bharat Sevashram Sangha activities was now truly established in Guyana, Trinidad and England. It was necessary to extend activities in North America. Sri Guruji Maharaj again showed the way. Guruji's devotees from Guyana and Trinidad who emigrated to Canada and the

USA, continued to practice their religion in these countries. They conducted Havan ceremony, as taught by Guruji, in their homes and later at rented accommodation for larger groups. It was evident that Guruji's influence was spreading into North America.

TORONTO ASHRAMS

A number of these devotees requested Guruji to send someone to start Sangha work in Toronto. In 1967, Swami Brahamanandaji responded to their request. Eventually a Temple was built in Royal Oak Road, Toronto by the selfless and dedicated efforts of Guruji's disciples and supporters. The Toronto Ashram was established performing weekly Havan service and celebrating Hindu Festivals. Swami Bhajanandaji was in charge for the Ashram for a period. Swami Puskaranandaji from India is currently responsible for a very popular and progressive Ashram. Swami Bhajanandaji is now in charge of another Ashram in Rivalda Road, Toronto. This Ashram is also popular and progressive with innovative activities to support the Hindu and other communities. On occasions, he seemed to try and emulate his Guruji particularly with activities and opportunities for young children.

NEW YORK ASHRAM

A similar situation arose in New York where disciples pleaded with Guruji to provide assistance to start a Sangha Ashram. Swami Vidyanandaji was sent to New York to promote the Ashram. Soon a large group of devotees raised funds and worked tirelessly to establish a Sangha Branch in Jamaica Queens, New York. Swami Vidyanandaji was in charge of this Ashram until 2015. Swami Shiveshwaranandaji took over responsibility and is currently in charge.

Swami Purnatmanandaji Maharai knew our Guruji ever since he was a young boy in India. He was full of respect and admiration for Guruji. particularly when he assisted Guruji at the Ashram in London for six months. He is currently President of the overseas Sangha branches. Swami Amarnatnandaji Maharaj also spent six months with Guruji at the London Ashram at a different period and was equally respectful. Having just joined the Sangha, Swami Amarnatnandaji clearly remembered when he first met Guruji on his visit to the Bankura Ashram. He was responsible to serve Guruji. These revered Swamis are currently in charge of Ashrams in the USA.

USA now has additional Sangha Ashrams in New Jersey, Los Angels and Chicargo with Milan Mandirs in Maryland and Minnesota. These Sangha Branches received extensive support from Hindus originally from Guyana , Trinidad and India.

Ever since February 1962, when Baroness Ravensdale, having been briefed by Guruji, spoke about Sri Guru Maharaj at the Maghi Purnima celebration at the London University, Guruji felt the Western appreciation of Hinduism. There is a hunger for our ancient knowledge and wisdom away from the popular ideas of yoga physical exercises. There are many English and American authors who have written many books on Hindu Philosophy, the Vedas, Upanishads and Vedanta. I personally experienced this desire for Hindu knowledge from a small group of ordinary American people who stopped me in a public park in San Francisco and politely engaged in over an hour of enquiring conversation on Yoga, reincarnation and meditation. Guruji tried to address this need in England with opportunities to expand his work to Holland, Belgium, Germany and Czechoslovakia. The USA offers good opportunities for expansion of Bharat Sevashram work. The Hindu community will continue to support Sri Guruji Maharaj's Sangha wherever it is established. That is the magnetism of the Sangha. It is a proud feeling to know that so many Sangha Centers are evolving in the USA and Canada. However, Guruji would be happy if his efforts to spread 'revived' Hinduism to Western people could be sustained in North America and other overseas countries.

BOOKS PUBLISHED BY GURUJI

These are some of the popular books published by Guruji.

1. Hindutwam in six different book sizes and eight revised editions.
2. Bhagwat Gita with easy translation and interpretation. Two revised editions.
3. A translation of Patanjali Yoga - collection of Yoga practices.
4. The Hinduism Journal (Published in London mainly for Western readers on aspects of Hinduism. Articles were written by people from various countries. The Journal had circulation to all Bharat Sevashram Sangha Ashrams and to European individuals and institutions.).
5. Prophet of a New Hindu Age. Life and teachings of Acharya Sri Guru Maharaj.
6. Yoga Devine Course.

Guruji wrote many articles for academic institutions and Inter Faith conferences.

PILGRIMAGE TRIPS TO INDIA

A very popular undertaken by overseas Sangha Ashrams was Pilgrimage trips to India. Swami Vidyanandaji and Swami Nirliptanandaji organized many group trips independently and at different times. Guruji's devotees from Guyana Trinidad, London, Canada and USA had opportunities to visit Sangha Ashrams, Shrines and Holy cities in India.

In 2007, Swami Nirliptanandaji arranged such a trip. I was among eight devotees and Swamiji in the group. It was a tough and exhausting but fascinating and spiritually invigorating experience for everybody. We visited many Bharat Sevashram Sangha Ashrams and holy cities from Hardwar to Chennai. The trip afforded us a chance to see the many holy places mentioned in the Ramayan and Mahabharat and brought to reality the stories in our scriptures.

However, my most personally rewarding experiences were at Maghi Purnima celebrations in Kolkata and a visit to the room of Sri Guruji Maharaj at Gaya Ashram. In a crowded auditorium of holy people and dignitaries during the evening celebrations of Maghi Purnima, I stood unobtrusively with my back against a wall when Swami Biswatmananadaji Maharaj approached me with a cloth in his hand and dusted off a table and asked me to sit on the table. After the main absorbing ceremony, I was on my way out to my lodgings when Swamiji again approached me and asked me to wait. He then came back with a bowl of Guru Maharaj's Prasad and insisted I ate it in front of him before I left. I was so surprised and could only reflect 'why me? a humble and unknown person' among a huge crowd of many prominent people. This act of consideration and kindness reminded me so much of our Guruji.

The other incident was in the Gaya Ashram. A Swamiji escorted myself and another devotee of our group to a room where Acharya Guruji Maharaj used to rest. As he unlocked the door and led us into the room, a strange cooling electrifying wave went through our bodies. The room was a shrine of Guru Maharaj. We prostrated ourselves in front of the 'Paduka' of Guru Maharaj with a silent personal prayer. Another reason for feeling fortunate was to be in a place where Guruji was at one time in charge.

A more recent Pilgrimage trip to Bajitpur, Bangladesh was organized mainly from Canada. It was equally exhilarating. A very devoted disciple of Guruji from Guyana and Canada desperately wanted to go on this trip. Regrettably, because of ill health he was unable to fulfill his dearest wish. People who have been fortunate to go on these Pilgrimage trips have benefited enormously spiritually and are grateful to the Swamis and organizers.

LONDON

The London Ashram continued its service to the community. The monthly Havan ceremony attracted large crowds sometimes up to one hundred and fifty people. The circulation of the journal 'Hinduism' increased. The publication of Guruji's book 'Prophet of a new Hindu Age' became an important final contribution. In his declining years and progressive poor health, Guruji concentrated on his life long desire to complete his work on the life of Acharya Guruji Maharaj and to bring His teachings in writing to the Western world. This would be a culmination of Guruji's many years of service in so many places in the world and a legacy for Bharat Sevashram Sangha, his disciples and devotees. The book was co-written with Professor Ninian Smart. Professor Smart's assistance, writing terminology and interpretation will help Western readers to appreciate the life and teachings of Sri Guru Maharaj. Since the short speech about Guru Maharaj by Baroness Ravensdale in1962, Guruji had this burning desire to present Sri Guru Maharaj to the Western public.

During the latter stages of publication, Guruji spent long hours preparing the manuscript at the London Ashram. He traveled many times to the Publisher in London dearly clutching the manuscript wrapped in a saffron cloth. A devotee offered to carry the bundle for him. Guruji refused. It was so precious that he constantly carried it closely pressed to his chest. Many devotees made generous donations for the very costly publication.

Guruji researched hundreds of Hindu names and address from United Kingdom telephone directories and posted leaflet information about the book. As the publication was nearly completed, Guruji became seriously ill and spent some anxious and worrying time in hospital. Fortunately he recovered. The book was published in 1985 and he visited Sangha devotees at his various Ashrams before returning to India. Less than one year later, Guruji left his mortal body on the 11th April 1986. In 1987 the London Ashram moved location from Stanlake Villas to Devonport Road within the same district of Shepherds Bush.

The London Ashram had many visits from Sangha monks from India, the West Indies and North America. London devotees had hoped that one Swamilj might have remained for longer periods to provide assistance to Swami Nirliptanandaji. A more recent visit in July 2019 was by a group of seven Sangha Swamijis from India under the leadership of Swami Saswapnanandaji Maharaj, Vice President of the Bharat Sevashram Sangha. The London Sangha devotees organized an elaborate religious programme over many days and at different venues to welcome the group. Nan and Ken Kowlessur are dedicated supporters of the London Ashram . Their generous and selfless assistance to Swami Nirliptanandaji and the Ashram is well known in Bharat Sevashram circles. They sponsored a two days Yagna ceremony at their residence in Suffolk, one hundred and twenty six miles from London, to welcome the Swamijis. Devotees from London and elsewhere attended a successful occasion and contributed a considerable sum of money as donation to a Swamiji who was building an International School in Delhi. Swami Saswapnanandaji was very complimentary about the work of the London Sangha devotees. He knew our Guruji and kept informed about his work overseas. He was also appreciative of our work to publish this book and offered his best wishes and blessings.

GURUJI'S EARLIER LIFE AND WORK

Very little was known about the life and work of Guruji before he arrived in Trinidad in December 1950. Many unsuccessful attempts were made to obtain the relevant information. During my visit to India in 2007, I visited several Sangha Ashrams in different states and spoke to many Brahmcharies and Swamijis who knew nothing or very little about Guruji. No one recognized any of the many photographs of Guruji I took with me. The early disciples of Sri Guruji Maharaj did not write or speak about themselves. Guruji Maharaj was the focal point of communication and importance. Photographs of these Holy Fathers demonstrated striking humility, resignation and devotion. Publicity or communication of personal information and achievements was irrelevant to these sanyasis. Guruji communicated some personal information of himself to his contemporary brother Swamiji only three months before he died. This was revealed only in context of a conversation about Guruji Maharaj.

In August 2011, I was fortunate to obtain some information from Mr. S. Chattergee who was from the same village where Guruji was born. Mr. Chaterjee was also very helpful to Guruji in the Stanlake Villas Ashram. Mr. S. Sinha, a professional Bengali, was also closely associated with Guruji in the London Ashram as well as with the Sangha Headquarter in Kolkata. Dinesh Sukhu arranged a meeting with Mr. Sinha to help me with my research on the early life of Guruji. Mr. Sinha was on his way to Calcutta for a holiday. He promised to go to the Sangha Headquarter and try to obtain information about Guruji. Mr. Sinha returned with an article written by a senior Sangha Swamiji exclusively on the early life and work of Guruji. I considered myself fortunate to obtain this article and other relevant information after years of research. Unfortunately the article was written in Bengali. Swaroop Das and Probeer Sarkar, devoted young students supporters of Bharat Sevashram Sangha in India and London, came to my rescue and helped with the translation of the Bengali documents.

As it is often difficult to translate or interpret the exact sentiment and meaning of another language and more particularly the Sanskrit vedic spiritual terminology, I ask the forgiveness of Guruji and Shree Guruji Maharaj, if I do not convey the information accurately. The following information is a partial translation of the article about our Guruji,.

Guruji was born on the 17th November 1905 to a moderately middle class family. He lived with his parents in a village named Nagar in Faridpur, East Bengal, currently Bangladesh. His father's name was Hara Kumar Sen Gupta. Guruji was named Bankin Sen Gupta.

His early school years were spent in the Nagpur district. Later he was a student at the reputable Upasi Higher Secondary School in Faridpur. Around the year 1921, he first heard about Guruji Maharaj from his close school friend Harsha Mukerjee. His teacher, Kshitish Chowdray, talked to him about Guruji Maharaj. Swami Suddhanandaji Maharaj also influenced him after many discussions about Guruji Maharaj.

In 1923, Guruji first met Guruji Maharaj in person at one of his preaching missions in Bhojeswar. Having completed his Matriculation examination, Guruji joined the

Bharat Sevashram Sangha in June1924. He was convinced that his future was in the hands of Guruji Maharaj and the Sangha. He was initially based at the Sangha headquarters in Boobazar street and in the vicinity of the current headquarters in Kalkota. Guruji was assigned to a preaching party under the leadership of Swami Bignanandaji Maharaj who also greatly influenced him in the formative years of his life as a Sanyasi of the Sangha.

The Sangha undertook two significant functions in its infancy. The first was to establish an infrastructural base for the organization to carry out the activities dictated by Guruji Maharaj. Consequently, the Sangha Headquarter was established. The other was the organization of Preaching Parties with responsibility for traveling to various parts of India to "re-invigorate Hinduism' and to raise funds for the Sangha. Eventually, the Sangha centers in Guyana, Trinidad, London and North America are the results of similar preaching parties.

In 1925, Guruji received his first spiritual initiation, possibly as a Brahmcharie as we know it. In 1928, Guruji received the 'Great Initiation' from Guruji Maharaj to become a Swamiji of the organization. Perhaps it is appropriate to mention here of an advice given to Guruji by Guruji Maharaj soon after Guruji decided to join the Sangha. This information is a translated extract from a letter Guruji wrote to his contemporary brother Swamiji in 1985, one year before Guruji departed from his mortal body. Guruji Maharaj advised, 'you must have strong determination to stay in the Ashram. You must have no contact with your friends or parents, no letters or correspondence, even if you become blind or paralyzed. Only by your own determination, spiritual discipline, steadfastness and dedication can you survive in the Ashram'. We are quite familiar with several examples of Guruji's determination, spiritual discipline, steadfastness and dedication to the wishes of Guruji Maharaj. I would like to add two further examples.

Guruji was always obedient, respectful and loving to his parents but more particularly to his mother. Even in his teenage years, he would ask his mother's permission to go to the toilet. Being an only son, he was idolized by his parents. Guruji's father had died before he went to the Ashram.

Approximately six months after joining the Sangha, Guruji met his mother by coincidence in Gaya. His mother and grandmother were in Gaya to perform the Shradah ceremony by the Ganges for his deceased father. Guruji was in the same location in Gaya with the Sangha preaching party. His mother was in tears pleading with Guruji to return to her and using heart felt words like 'who would look after your widowed mother?' and 'why don't you kill me?' This must have been an extremely moving and testing experience for both of them. It was Guruji's powerful determination and the blessing of Guruji Maharaj that influence his decision to remain in the Ashram. In his letter, Guruji indicated that he survived this encounter through the 'Victory and Glory' of Guruji Maharaj.

The other incident was in 1942. Guruji was on flood relief work in the district of Barisal since 1941 helping, rescuing and feeding victims of the flood. There was also a major riot between Hindus and Muslims in 1942. Many people were killed in the riots that extended as far as the city of Dhaka. Many Hindus were displaced and left their homes and possessions. People moved to different districts up to Agartala in Assam.

Thousands of refugees sought relative shelter and safety around the Akhura railway station with a measure of protection from the Bharat Sevashram Sangha. Guruji was assigned to lead a relief work group for the displaced and desolate victims of the riots and persecution. The Government at that time enforced 'Law 114' to restore control and order. A curfew was ordered which forbade a gathering or meeting of more than four people. The atmosphere was volatile, depressing and even hostile. Additionally, people experienced sadness, hunger and sickness. Guruji's task was formidable and presented a massive challenge. It took great courage and determination to conduct the Sangha's activities under these circumstances.

Guruji organized a prayer meeting, performed a Havan ceremony and arranged for people to be fed. A huge 'bale' tree was stripped bare of its leaves for the ceremony. Fruits and 'prasad' were piled up in a mound 'so high that you could hardly see over it'. It was estimated that more than one hundred thousand people attended the ceremony. Guruji overcame all apparent obstacles and to some extent, defied the curfew law. The police came in large numbers not to object or arrest, but to protect and help control the large gathering. The activities of Guruji helped to boost the morale of the refugees. Most of them returned to their homes and villages.

Guruji moved around several Sangha Ashrams in India. He helped in building new Ashrams and managing existing ones. One senior and elderly Sangha Swamiji remembered Guruji successfully in charge of the large and very busy Sangha Ashram in Gaya. Guruji occasionally recalled the treasured time he worked and spent with Swami Advaitanandaji and Swami Vedanandaji, two of his contemporary Holy Fathers of the Sangha.

In all aspects of Guruji's work, one will find a consistently disciplined dedication to duty and the wishes of Guruji Maharaj. He endured sacrifice and personal hardships on several occasions. He slept on the ground of a piece of land donated to him for a school building. When it rained, he sat up and sheltered under an umbrella. He survived on eating dried coconut and drinking liquid he made from boiled papaya leaves. He lived in huts and 'cow sheds' horribly exposed to the elements. He ate basic Ashram food and fasted for days on many occasions. There were many more examples of severe personal sacrifices. In later years his health declined.

I would like to refer to an article written by Swami Dibyanandaji Maharaj on two incidents in Guruji's life that encompasses his immense Sangha Spirituality. In 1985, Guruji was seriously ill in London and taken to the Hammersmith Hospital. Many devotees did not expect him to survive. Guruji himself felt his end was near. He instructed his closest devotees that donated money for the publication of his book, must be returned to the donor if he passed away. Swami Dibyanandaji wrote that during the night, Guruji Maharaj appeared before him and told him 'Purnananda, you have done a lot in the West. You go and visit Guyana, Trinidad, Canada and America and meet all the devotees and encourage them to continue the Sangha activities. Then come back to London and finally come to Mother India, then I will take you'. Guruji made a rapid recovery by the blessings of

Guruji Maharaj and subsequently went on to complete his last mission as directed by Guruji Maharaj.

The other incident was during his final days in Kolkata Headquarters. Guruji returned to India before Maghi Purnima in 1986. He was in good health. He took part in Maghi Purnima and Shivratri celebrations. In March 1986, some other senior Swamijis asked Guruji to accompany them to the Kumbhmela celebrations in Hardwar. Guruji replied, 'I will not go, I am in Guru Maharaj's Siddhipath, this is my Hardwar, this is my Kumbhmela'.

On the 11thApril 1986 at 1745 hrs, His Holiness Srimat Swami Purnandaji Maharaj gave up his mortal body at the Holy feet of Guruji Maharaj at the 'Sanctum Sanctorum', in the Kolkata Sangha Headquarters.

Our Guruji was an exceptional man, a great saint and a unique Sanyasi. There will never be another person like Swami Purnananndaji Maharaj. He influenced the lives of thousands of people from different background. Although he is no longer with us in person, many of his devotees continue to experience the spiritual values of his intervention in their lives.

TRIBUTES TO GURUJI AND HIS WORK

The following tributes by a few prominent devotees who worked for Guruji enhanced the greatness of our Guruji:

Guruji was a tower of strength, a beacon of light, a confidant, a source of solace, a healing balm, a person to go to when all else failed. He was an embodiment of the mythical 'Benevolent King' Nowrang Persaud.

This 'God-man's' life must be seen as an offering in the service of humanity. When the History of Guyana is properly written, the name of Swami Purnananda must occupy a prominent and esteemed place and should be written in gold. Saisnarine Kowlesar.

We must accept that Guru Maharaj had sent Guruji to take us, His children, unto Him. Guruj Maharaj will continue to inspire and unite the devotees of the Sangha. When Guruji made his final departure from Guyana, his devotees asked Guruji, 'How can we honour you for what you have done for us?' Guruji replied, 'express your gratitude to Guruji Maharaj. I am the instrument of Guru Maharaj. He did his work through this instrument. All that I have done was through the Divine Grace and Glory of Guru Maharaj'. Swami Dibyanandaji

Swami Purnanandaji Maharaj was a monk of the highest order. He was a direct disciple of Swami Prananvanandaji Maharaj (Guru Maharajji) and reflected the Great Master in his behavior and interactions with others. He was strong, bold, forceful and a tremendous spiritual force. He had attained great spiritual heights through intense sadhana but for all that, he was ever humble. 'Everything I have ever achieved, and I am not far from moksha', I heard him said many years ago, 'is because of the padukas (slippers) of Guru Maharaj'. He had totally surrendered his life to Satguru and Satguru's grace was ever with him, I doubt we will ever see the likes of him again in the West. He was truly a spiritual giant. Swami Shiveshwarannandaji.

Very many thanks to all of you for your services to Swami Purnanandaji Maharaj and The Bharat Sevashram Sangha. Swami Saswapnanandaji Maharaj, (Vice President of The Bharat Sevashram Sangha, on his visit to London, 15th July 2019).

I would like to mention a few additional truths about Guruji. He never wrote or spoke about himself and his achievements. I may incur his displeasure for writing so much about his life and work.

Guruji never 'preached' to individual or groups of people. He offered interpretations and lessons from the Scriptures, particularly from the Bhagawat Gita, the Ramayan, the Vedas and the words of Guruji Maharaj.

Many of his disciples and devotees will remember at least one special interaction with our Guruji. What one will never forget, either as an individual or as a member of a large audience, is the manner in which he first greeted one. Guruji, with an endearing smile, would clasp his hands, humbly bow his head as if in prayer, and demonstrated genuine respect and appreciation. This gesture was always expressed when devotees placed a flowered 'mala' (garland) on him. Guruji never wore this garland for long. He would remove it as soon as it was convenient and place it at the Altar of Guruji Maharaj. He demonstrated that the honour and respect of the devotees was for Guruji Maharaj and not for him.

In his memory, I would like to express a personal tribute, hoping that it also represents the sentiments of many of his devotees and supporters.

Guruji, your hard work, dedication, sacrifices and personal suffering provided us with a renewed perception of practical Hinduism. You gave us formal education, knowledge, confidence and personal beliefs, all maturing into many wonderful individual achievements. You left us a legacy, tangible, spiritual and unparallel in modern times. Your Sangha Centers in Guyana, Trinidad, USA and Canada continue to flourish on Sangha principles and are fervently supported by thousands of your devotees. These centers are our heritage.

Like a father, you nurtured, protected and loved us. You forgave our mistakes and empathized with our shortcomings. You embraced, comforted and consoled us and often demonstrated a genuine concern for our personal welfare and spiritual well being.

A true Guru is a Guru for eternal life – beyond this life, beyond reincarnations, beyond this Kali Yuga and all other Yugas. Guruji, you are that Guru. Your disciples and devotees will have at least one special memory. It may be your smile, a laugh, even an angry gesture, an embrace or a blessing from your hand – a hand that anointed the Holy feet of Sri Guruji Maharaj. Sometimes this moment can be impossible to describe or is so special and valuable, that it is perhaps better to remain a private experience. This memory can serve as a beacon light of energy that offers us consolation in times of sorrow and peace and happiness in times of celebration.

I know I risk your displeasure for this tribute as you often remarked that you are only the instrument of Sri Guruji Maharaj's wishes. We therefore feel fortunate to be the beneficiaries of the wishes of Sri Guruji Maharaj and participants in his great organization, the Bharat Sevashram Sangha.

Above all Guruji, through you we learn about the Grace of Guruji Maharaj. As we do not ask for, but still receive the life sustaining heat of the sun and the air we breathe, similarly our lives have been nourished and influenced by Guruji Maharaj. You gave us the opportunity to sing the praises of Guruji Maharaj and hopefully to be within easy reach of his blessings and protection. The future children of The Bharat Sevashram Sangha will certainly benefit from the legacy you left us. Guruji, you are indeed our mother and father.

For all that you have given us we are eternally grateful. We bow down before you in utmost humility.

His Holiness Swami Purnanandaji Maharaj

Early, in Guyana

Later, in London

In a temple for Early Holy Fathers at Puri Ashram, India

Om akhanda manda laakaram vyaptamyena
cha raa chraram.
Tat padam Darshitam yena tasmai Sri Gurave namah.

I bow down before Gurudeva who has
revealed to me the Lotus feet of the Almighty
who is the all-pervasive Infinite Being.

BIBLIOGRAPHY

Vedananda, Swami, Bharat Sevashram Sangha Activity Report. Kolkatta,India, 1952.

Vedananda, Swami, The Prophet of the Age, Kolkata, India, 1997.

Smart, Ninian & Purnananda, Swami, Prophet of a New Hindu Age, London, George Allen & Unwin, 1985.

Advaitananda, Swami, Letter, Bharat Sevashram Sangha, Ahmedabad, India, 1966.

Akshayananda, Swami, Letter, Bharat Sevashram Sangha, Gaya, India, 1965.

Nirmalananda, Swami, Letter, Bharat Sevashram Sangha. Kolkata, India, 1965.

Yatishwarananda, Swami, Letter, Bharat Sevashram Sangha. Ahmedabad, India, 1965.

Dibyananda, Swami, Feature Article, Revival of Hinduism in the West, Trinidad, (nd).

Purnananda, Swami, Bhagawat Gita Translated, Trinidad, 1955.

Kowlesar, Saisnarine, feature Article, Swami Purnananda, An unsung Hero, Guyana, 1995.

Singh, Dr. Lake, Portrait of a Saint, His Holiness Swami Purnananda Maharaji, Brampton, Canada, 2011.

Persaud, Nowrang, A personal interaction with Swami Purnanandaji, Guyana, (nd).

****